How Can I Help?

How Can I Help?

Reaching Out to Someone Who Is Grieving

June Cerza Kolf

BAKER BOOK HOUSE
Grand Rapids, Michigan 49516

Copyright 1989 by
Baker Book House Company

ISBN: 0-8010-5276-9

Second printing, May 1991

Printed in the United States of America

The following are acknowledged for
permission to quote from their copyrighted material:

Little Brown and Company: *A Gift of Hope* by Robert Veninga
Harper & Row: *To Conquer Loneliness* by Harold Blake Walker
Verna Diggs: "Reflecting on Widowhood"
Larry Richards and Paul Johnson: "Death and the Caring Community"
J. Grand Swank: "The Bright Side of Pain"

Scripture quotations are taken from *The Living Bible* © 1971 by
Tyndale House Publishers, Wheaton, IL 60187

To protect the privacy of the persons with whom the author is
associated, many names and situations have been changed or disguised.

To my mother,
Olga Cerza,
who taught me by example,
—not with words—
all about love, grief, and acceptance

Contents

Death is not putting out the light.
It is
extinguishing the candle
because the dawn has come.

Preface

I looked up from reading the obituary column of our local newspaper.

"Oh, my goodness, Henry Johnson's wife has died. I'll have to call him right away," I told my husband. His expression clearly indicated that he thought I had lost my mind.

"Don't you think you should give him a few days before you call?" he questioned me.

Before becoming employed by a hospice organization and working with their bereavement-support group, I, too, would have waited a few days, sent a sympathy card, and avoided anyone who was grieving. However, I have learned an entirely new set of rules from working with grieving people.

I have learned that it is essential to make contact as soon as possible. I have been told that the support of others in the first hours of grief is the most valuable gift we can give. Therefore I knew it was necessary to get in touch with Henry immediately to let him know that I was hurting with him. At the same time I needed to find out how I could be of assistance. There was no other way to accomplish these tasks than by phoning or going to his house. I decided to phone.

I was surprised when Henry answered the telephone himself. I explained that I had just seen the obituary and that I was very sorry. In this particular situation it was Henry who was my friend not his wife. I had only met her on several brief occasions. Therefore, my concern was for him, rather than experiencing the personal loss his wife's death would make in my own life.

Henry sounded genuinely pleased to hear from me. I could hear him catch his breath when I offered my condolences, and he interrupted me in midsentence.

"Craziest thing you ever saw," he told me in his heavy southern accent. "We were sitting there watching television when Betty said she felt funny, grabbed her chest, and fell over."

This was obviously a time when the bereaved person needed to talk about the actual death before beginning to believe it himself. I encouraged him by asking simple questions without probing beyond anything he wished to offer. I purposely did not tell him he should try not to think about it. I did not offer any advice. I just listened with an occasional "uh-huh." I definitely did not interrupt to share a similar story. I tried not to act shocked or distressed by what he was saying.

Any of those reactions would have given him the unspoken message that I could not handle his grief. It would have shut the door that needed to be opened in order to air out the shock of a sudden death. Each time he told the story, he would be able to grasp the facts a bit more, until at last he too would know his wife was gone.

Henry went into great detail about the way Betty looked. The details were not pleasant to hear, but I had called him to help him. Listening was the best way I could do that. When it became obvious that he was finished with the details of the death, I steered the conversation toward the plans for the next few days.

Talking about funeral-home visitations, memorial services, or cemeteries are all subjects we usually avoid. Henry needed to talk about these details before he could face the next three days. He had to verbally walk along the path many times so that when he physically approached the new terrain, he would be able to find his way. I led him with an occasional question, being careful not to invade his privacy.

Then I asked about the household situation. Henry told me that he had many out-of-town guests. If he had been alone, I would have immediately gone to be with him until family members arrived. I inquired about the length of time these people would be staying. Did anyone else need to be picked up from the airport? These questions let me know whether help was needed in practical matters. As we talked, I was mentally asking myself if I was needed for transportation, extra bedding, or a foldout cot. Would a meal be required after the funeral?

I was not merely being curious; I was planning my strategy as we talked. It sounded like Henry had everything under control at the present time and that his greatest need was going to come one week later, when his family returned to their own homes.

I hastily jotted Henry's name on my calendar as I told him I would be attending the funeral. Then I told him that I hoped to see him after all his company left.

"Why don't you pencil me in on your calendar for lunch on March third, and I'll talk to you the day before to confirm our plans," I told him.

My reason for doing this was so that Henry would have something concrete to look forward to after he was left alone.

Then I told him I would be praying for him and his family. When I hung up the phone, I headed straight for my Bible and added Henry's name to my prayer list, so that I would remember the prayers I had promised.

The following day I sent a sympathy card. Although I had not known Henry's wife well, I did have a couple of vivid memories of her. I not only signed my name to the card, I also wrote about these memories on the blank side.

When I attended the funeral, I was generous with hugs for all the family—even the members I had not met before. As I approached Henry in the receiving line, I hugged him tightly and reminded him of our date for lunch. It was one of the few smiles I saw that day.

"I'll be saving up my appetite just for that," he replied.

At home I continued my prayers. A week later, I called Henry to confirm our lunch date. At that time I asked him to tell me honestly if he felt like going out. He said he did. If he had sounded hesitant, I would have suggested taking lunch over to his house instead, or I would have invited him to my house for homemade soup. There are times when the survivor is not up to facing a restaurant because he fears running into people unexpectedly. It is important to be sensitive to the individual needs in each situation.

As soon as we were seated for lunch, I opened the conversation with, "It must be very different for you living alone after all these years. How are you getting along so far?" Being specific is better than the general question, "How are you doing?"

We talked much more than we ate. Henry mentioned that he appreciated my phone call and especially my interest in Betty's death.

"Nobody else was letting me talk about the way Betty died.

Every time I would start to talk about it, they would pat me and say, 'There, there.' I was so glad you wanted to hear all the details."

To be perfectly honest, I had *not* wanted to hear all the details, but I knew from working with other bereaved persons the importance of grievers' being able to repeat the details again and again.

Later that afternoon, Henry mentioned how glad he was for our date on the calendar. It had been a goal for him to aim toward. He said it had been helpful for him to not be faced with a calendar of blank days. It made him realize that plans could still be made and life could still go on, even if his wife of forty-seven years was gone.

During lunch I brought up the subject of the funeral. Again I tried to be specific in my remarks. "The funeral was very nice. I really liked the one white rose in Betty's hand. And the minister's message was very touching."

Henry nodded and began to tell me how difficult it had been to plan a funeral. Few people had affirmed that the funeral had gone smoothly and that it had been a proper farewell to Betty. The death had been such a shock that Henry was worrying about whether he had made the proper decisions. I reassured him that he had done a superb job, especially under the circumstances.

That day, Henry went over the details of the actual death one more time. The story sounded as if it were on a tape recorder. Obviously this was a "tape" that Henry needed to play. I listened to the story again.

Henry is hard of hearing. I feel certain that the people at nearby tables could not possibly understand the nature of our discussion. To them, it must have sounded terribly morbid and may have even ruined some appetites. For that, I am truly sorry, but we were in the process of working through grief. Talking about the death plays a great part in the process. Grief does not go away if it is ignored or put on the back shelf. Grief needs to be faced and it takes hard work before it can be accepted.

In the year since Betty's death, I have heard the story of her death repeatedly. Henry no longer cries when he plays the tape and he is beginning to shorten it. I know soon he will move away from it completely as acceptance takes place.

I also notice that Henry is again laughing heartily, and the twinkle has returned to his eyes. When he talks about Betty, it is to recall the happy times and to share the crazy experiences they had as cattle ranchers. At this point, I am encouraging him to talk about those happy memories.

Henry is quick to hug me and tell me I was a big help to him. It is very rewarding to see his progress and to know that I played a part in it. While I was helping him, I was learning to be comfortable with death. Now when I am faced with losses of my own, I will hopefully be able to deal with them more easily.

I was not always comfortable with death. Until three years ago my own family had seemed exempt. Then in a short time period, five family members and two close friends were taken from us in death. At this same time, I was co-leading a bereavement-support group and was therefore experiencing my own grief, as I was reaching out to help others handle theirs. Together we learned, grew, and accepted. As a result of this, I realized that society plays a large role in our acceptance of grief and how quickly that acceptance comes about. The quality of the support a person receives when a loved one dies can help or hinder grief work tremendously.

Although every death is different and each griever is a

unique person, there are many common ways that comfort can be offered. It is my desire to share this information in the hopes that it will give more people the necessary confidence to reach out and ease the pain of someone they care about.

PART 1

The Initial Contact

1

Responding to the News

When we receive the news that someone we know has died, we experience various reactions as our mind works quickly to assimilate the information. Some of the feelings we may experience are shock, anger, guilt, or just profound, heart-wrenching sadness. As we sort through these mixed feelings, we begin to think about the loved ones who have been left to grieve this loss. We hurt for them. We want to do something— anything—to help ease their pain. Unfortunately we usually do not know what to do.

It is of utmost importance to make contact as soon as possible. Human contact in the early hours of grief seems to be the most important factor. Strength and support for the grieving are drawn from merely leaning toward others, just as a plant leans toward the rays of light for survival, strength, and growth. Naturally there are times when distance makes it impossible to physically go to the grieving people. In these situations a phone call or a letter can be sent without hesitation. When distance is not a problem, we should assess the situation, and if we feel led to go to the bereaved people, we must go at once.

Each time death has touched my life I have been surprised at the people who came to offer comfort. They were never the people I had expected. At first I felt let down and disappointed in those friends and relatives who did not respond at my time of grief. Hindsight has shown me that those particular people would not have been able to cope with my sorrow. Often close friends are grieving so intensely themselves that they hesitate to approach the bereaved family. They have nothing of themselves to offer. Instead God sends special people to fill our voids effectively and efficiently. For this reason it is important to listen for the small, quiet voice that may be giving us instructions.

"Comfort, oh comfort my people says your God" (Isa. 40:1). The word comfort comes from two Latin words "com" and "fortis" meaning, "strengthened by being with." When death arrives, a great need for comfort also arrives. Frequently family members are unable to support each other because of their own intense grief. An outside person (who can look at the situation from a short distance) can offer resources, energy, and strength that is depleted in the main grievers. A good example of this is shown by statistics on parents who have suffered the devastating death of a child. The divorce rate with these couples is extremely high. Instead of holding each other up, they seem to pull each other down. One social worker compared it to two bent sticks. In a bent, anguished position no support is possible.

One parent explained that when he is having a good day and coming up to the surface for air, his spouse may be fighting to keep from drowning. The frantic clinging can pull the first person back down. This causes resentment, which in turn results in anger, guilt, and a myriad of negative feelings. Therefore we must not assume that we are not needed because there are plenty of family members available. Outside help can still be valuable and should be gently offered. Our personal presence cannot be replaced with any amount of floral bouquets, casseroles, or sympathy cards. There is a certain warmth—a certain soothing effect—that comes only in the form of human contact. The touch of a warm hand, the hug from a strong arm, and the shared tears are all consoling.

I personally became aware of the importance of physical support by a touching gesture made by one of my nephews the day of my mother-in-law's funeral. It was a typical frigid November day in Illinois with the thermometer never reaching as high as ten degrees. My husband and I were foolishly dressed in our warmest California clothing, which consisted of only a lightweight coat for me and a business suit for him. The wind was howling across the deserted cemetery, and the ground was so frozen that it crunched and crackled under our feet as we stepped out of the car.

Our nephew assisted us in getting out of the car. But instead of walking away he surprised us by opening his topcoat, putting an arm around each of us and tucking us close to his body. He is a big hulk of a guy who could easily huddle us both inside his overcoat for protection against the wind. We stood that way throughout the graveside service. I never tell this story without getting choked up and my eyes filling with tears. It was not the physical warmth provided by David that was most important. No, it was the shelter of his loving thoughtfulness that touched us and eased our pain. I thank God for moments and memories of generations reaching out to each other in times of need.

Karl Menninger has said the central purpose of each individual's life should be to dilute the misery in the world. Every day each of us is offered opportunities to do just that—sometimes in large ways, sometimes in small—sometimes by wrapping our relatives in our overcoats at a cemetery! Instead we often let inertia, fear, or selfishness stop us. Going at once to grieving people is one way to dilute the misery in the world. It may upset our plans and throw off our schedules, but the personal rewards we receive from helping others will make it worthwhile.

In his book *A Gift of Hope,* Robert Veninga tells about surviving the losses and the heartbreaks that life sometimes brings. He interviewed over a hundred people while trying to come to a conclusion on how people were able to withstand devastating tragedies in their lives. One important discovery he made was this:

> Almost without exception those who survive a tragedy give credit to one person who stood by them, supported them, and gave a sense of hope. If you want to survive a tragedy, you need a friend. At least that is the experience of most individuals who have withstood some of the stiffest challenges that life can bring.
>
> Kahlil Gibran once remarked that we can forget those with whom we have laughed, but we can never forget those with whom we have cried. Most friendships worth their salt are those nourished in human struggle. Once you have suffered together, there is a bond that is not severed by the passage of time.[1]

Louise Carroll writes about a grieving person, "Through his tears he may not see clearly, but his heart will be warmed by the human touch and loving care. Later he may not remember what was said, but he will remember the warmth and closeness. He will remember there were those who cared. Over his sadness will be a mist of love, and it will help him through his difficult time."[2]

How can we create a "mist of love"? We can create it with sincere concern, a willingness to help, sincere prayers, and our physical presence whenever possible.

2

Offering Condolences

It is difficult to know what to say during the first contact with someone who is grieving. We often avoid grievers because we feel we lack the right words. There are no pat speeches and no perfect words. Instead, we need to simply say what is in our hearts. Sometimes a hug or a squeeze of the hand can better express what we are feeling than words. As I asked grieving people to share with me any messages that had been especially meaningful, I was told repeatedly that they could not remember actual comforting words, but they could list every single person who had stayed near them that first day.

More important than any particular action or word of advice was the simple presence of someone who cared. When someone says to us in the midst of a crisis, "I do not know what to say or what to do, but I want you to realize that I am with you, that I will not leave you alone," we have a friend through whom we can find consolation and comfort.[3]

When we go to grieving people, we must go with compassion. Luke 6:36 asks us to "Try to show as much compassion as your Father does" (TLB). "Compassion asks us to go where it hurts, to enter into places of pain, to share in brokenness, fear, confusion and anguish. Compassion challenges us to cry out with those in misery, to mourn with those who are lonely, to weep with those in tears. Compassion requires us to be weak with the weak, vulnerable with the vulnerable, and powerless with the powerless."[4]

Often being compassionate means not saying anything at all. When Job of the Old Testament was having all his troubles, three of his friends came by and "sat upon the ground with him silently for seven days and nights with no one speaking a word; for they saw that his suffering was too great for words" (Job 2:13). The suffering of grief can be too intense for words.

I witnessed a similar situation one time as I watched a pastor arrive at the scene of a death. After he had gone to pray with the family by the bedside of the deceased, he came into the living room and took off his jacket and tie. Then he sat down in a rocking chair, and did not say a word.

We could all tell at a glance that he had settled in to stay and that our job was completed. There was no need for our hospice team to linger any longer. He would be taking care of the bereaved wife until other family members arrived. He brought not words, but compassion to that home.

Likewise the night of my uncle's wake a young man showed up and introduced himself as a student that my uncle had taught in junior high school ten years before. The man said that my uncle had been a good man and a good teacher. Then he sat in a chair off to the side of the room and remained there the entire four hours. At the end of the evening, he knelt before the casket quietly and then left. I found this very touching, as did other family members. This young man had not needed to speak during those long, dreary hours. His presence spoke louder than words.

I am often asked if it is not morbid to want to be with someone who has just experienced the death of a loved one. People want to know why I continue to work with the dying and the grieving. Don't I find it terribly depressing? No, it is not depressing to work with these people; it is surprisingly uplifting and rewarding. To be able to reach out my hand to someone who is struggling with one of the heaviest loads life can offer, making it a tiny bit lighter, brings about a genuine feeling of accomplishment. Mother Teresa claims she finds Jesus with the poorest of the poor. I find Jesus with people who are grieving as he furnishes me with the words and actions to help them.

As a result of my work, my own life has been changed. I have become very aware of my own mortality. I waste less time over trivial matters. I appreciate every day as never before, and I am continually amazed at how blessed I am. A car that will not start in the morning, a checkbook that will not balance, a roof that leaks, an irritable husband, or a moody teenaged daughter, seem inconsequential compared to the burdens I see people carrying every single day. So I willingly leave my pleasant life to go where the pain has settled. I know from personal experience how important it is to have the support of others in a time of grief, so I actively look for opportunities to offer that type of comfort to others.

3

Clichés

fter speaking with many grieving people, I have learned that the time following the loss of a loved one is definitely not a time for clichés. Popular clichés such as: "Time heals everything"; "Count your blessings"; "Try to look for the good in this situation"; "Your loved one is happier with the Lord"; and "She is through suffering at last" do not seem to help at all.

An entire book has been written about such clichés, titled "*I Know Just How You Feel . . . avoiding the clichés of grief*" by Erin Linn. In 1974, Mrs. Linn's six-year-old son was hit by a car and killed instantly. She states that "through years of work with bereaved people and of hearing the desperate plight of those who want to comfort the bereaved, I am convinced that the misunderstandings that exist between the two can be avoided." From her book, I have compiled a list of clichés and the statements that would be more helpful.

Meaningless Cliché	**Positive Statement**
Time will heal.	You must feel as if this pain will never end.
It's a blessing.	I'm sorry this had to happen.
God never gives us more than we can handle.	This must seem like more than you can handle.
You must be strong.	Don't feel you need to be strong for me.
You're holding up so well.	It's okay to cry.
This is God's will.	Some things just don't make any sense.
I know how you feel.	I just don't know what to say.
Let me know if I can do anything.	I'll call tomorrow to see how I can help.[5]

When the wound of death is fresh and tender, clichés are simply too pat, too superficial. Instead of clichés, grieving people need to hear reassurances that their suffering is genuine and that the life of the deceased loved one stood for something. If words seem to be required, a simple remark such as, "I'm so very sorry," or a specific comment such as, "I'll miss having Jim holler 'good morning' to me when I go out and get my newspaper. He was such a cheerful neighbor!" Or, "Church bazaars will never be the same without Janet; she was always the one with the creative ideas that made those events a success" are better choices than clichés.

Statements which validate that a void has been made on this earth, or simply that the deceased person will be missed are all statements that are appreciated. Short, meaningful memories that can be shared or photographs are also special.

For example, following my dad's memorial service, while we

were having refreshments, a neighbor came up to me smiling sheepishly. He said, "This may be totally inappropriate but I have a slide of your mom and dad that I want you to see." Then he reached into his jacket pocket, pulled out a small slide viewer, and handed it to me. Inside was a slide taken of my parents the year before in the same room of the church where we were presently standing. Mom and Dad were smiling and obviously having a wonderful time. It warmed my heart to see this picture, and I knew it was Gordon's loving way of reminding me of the good times my parents had shared. It also brought to mind a picture of my dad as happy and healthy versus the picture that I had of him during his last few days of life.

No, it was not inappropriate at all. It was a beautiful gesture and one I treasure. It put a personal touch on the loss we were all suffering and validated the life that had once been. It is one of the few things I remember about that day. Gordon went on to order enlargements of that photograph for all the members of the family and had them sent to us. I am very appreciative of that.

When we want to help grievers, we need to allow them time to grieve and not try to brush off their loss as inconsequential. Our desire should be to open doors that will let the light of understanding and hope trickle in, rather than just slamming the door shut by saying the wrong thing. If we sometimes stumble, stammer, and say something wrong, the survivors realize how awkward we are feeling. If something dreadful should come out of our mouth, we can simply admit it and say, "Oh, that wasn't what I meant to say to you at all. I just feel so awkward and I hurt so much for you." Honesty is appreciated.

When the loss suffered is a child, it is best not to say, "Be glad you have other children," or "You're young; you can have another child." Each child is special, and no child replaces another. These comments tend to make grieving parents angry and can be extremely devastating. They may also isolate the bereaved people even further from society and make them feel as if nobody—anywhere—understands their agony.

"God needed another angel" is not soothing nor is it biblically sound. I do not believe a loving God would destroy a family or place such devastating despair into the hearts of the parents. "Be grateful for the time you had little Johnny" is also not a positive statement. Grieving parents cannot be grateful for anything. Expecting parents to express gratitude at such a time is unrealistic and can actually bring about guilt. It is more appropriate to tell the couple that we will miss the joy their child brought us and that our heart aches for them. We do not need to feel embarrassed if we begin to cry in their presence. It will only reassure them that we do truly care.

Because the loss of a child goes against nature, society does not know of any way to deal with it. Frank Deford, whose eight-year-old daughter died of cystic fibrosis wrote in *Alex,* "Old people die with achievements, memories. Children die with opportunities, dreams" (Viking Press).

Those of us who have not experienced the death of a child feel at a complete loss. Therefore, we must encourage people who have previously had this agonizing experience to be the ones to do the reaching out. Because of their personal heartache they are the only ones who can truly understand and embrace the newly broken heart. When their own wound has healed, they will experience inner peace when they can put their own senseless loss to a purpose by providing comfort to someone else with a similar hurt.

I watched a good example of this when one of our bereavement-support groups contained a lovely young couple whose three-year-old son had died suddenly of congenital heart failure. A year later the mother and a hospital social worker asked me to help them set up a support group for bereaved parents. The group is now meeting on a regular basis. The bereaved mother claims it was the healthiest thing she could have done. She feels she is bringing about a bit of good from her little son's otherwise meaningless death. Currently this young mother is also on a list at the local hospital, so she will be called anytime day or night that a young child dies in the hospital. She wants to be notified so that she can go to the aid of the parents. In her reaching out to help others, her own grief is fading and diminishing.

4

Assistance in Practical Matters

In addition to our physical presence, everyday tasks may need to be done for the grieving family. When tasks need doing, we should simply do them, rather than ask, "Should I tidy up the house?" Unless it requires a major decision, we can quietly go about the job. Linens may need to be changed for out-of-town guests, and transportation may need to be provided. Clothes for the funeral may need to be pressed or taken to the cleaners. The tasks we can tackle will depend on our closeness to the bereaved. Naturally we would not open closets or begin to use the washing machine at the home of a mild acquaintance. We have to choose what is suitable in each situation.

If this is a family we do not know very well, but we still wish to help, food is always appreciated. However, we need to keep in mind that the grieving household is generally deluged with desserts or casseroles. It is best to choose something more original, such as homemade soup, cold meats and rolls for quick lunches, or a coffee cake for breakfast. We must always remember to mark any containers that need to be returned with our names and possibly even our phone numbers. It is easy to forget where the dish came from in the confusion of a disrupted household. Disposable containers are even better.

A friend told me that several hours after her father had died, she answered a knock on the door. There stood a neighbor with a large, battered kettle in her hands.

"This is for you," the neighbor said and quickly left.

My friend lifted the lid and said that her nostrils were assaulted with the most delicious aroma. In the pot was a thick, rich soup made from chunks of carrots, hunks of tender meat, barley, green beans, and even pieces of tomato all combined in a thick, rich brown broth.

During the next few days that pot was on the stove almost constantly. From it came a dinner for two that first evening, when nobody had felt like cooking but their stomachs were growling nevertheless. It provided a filling, hot, midnight snack one night when she could not sleep. And she had it bubbling on the stove, making the house smell inviting, when her brother arrived after a late night flight. The soup was not only nourishing and easy to serve, but it brought with it a feeling of being loved and pampered as only homemade soup can do.

Another time, I was involved with a grieving family when a friend brought over sliced French rolls, a variety of lunch meats, sliced cheese, and a jar of mayonnaise. With it, she brought a big jug of iced tea and a package of paper plates, cups, and napkins. It made meal preparation simple for the large crowd of people staying in one house. People ate when they became hungry. When you are dealing with jet lag and different time zones, meals can become a major ordeal. Something easy that can be prepared quickly is greatly appreciated.

In addition to food, transportation assistance is often a necessity. Although people who are grieving are easily distracted, they are not aware of this. They will insist they can drive and attempt other tasks, such as lighting a fire in a fireplace, that can prove to be dangerous. Watch for these possible dangers and take over the task if it looks like a potential problem.

After my father died, my mother appeared surprisingly capable of functioning. I was continually surprised by the calm way that she made decisions, carried out chores, and accomplished tasks. Looking back, I realize that she was experiencing some shock (just as I was) and only *looked* capable. Six months later she told me that she had no recollection of that time period in her life.

The day after Dad died she had insisted that we needed to go to the bank, and I had foolishly agreed to drive her there. We were a regular Laurel and Hardy as I drove in the pelting rain to a place I had never been before.

When she told me to turn, I was already past the parking lot entrance. I tried to go around the block but all I could find were one-way streets. I managed to get all twisted around before finding the bank a second time. We got soaking wet running from the car to the bank and found ourselves laughing in spite of ourselves as a release to the stress. Once inside the bank, the teller had been extremely rude as Mom fumbled and dropped the bank book. Mom gave her the wrong completed form, which was soaking wet. The teller had sighed and been cranky in explaining the error.

I had been tempted to inform the teller that she was dealing with an eighty-year-old woman who had not been out of the house for two months and whose husband had just died. Then I remembered to "turn the other cheek" and had to bite my tongue as tears filled my eyes. Maybe the people during the

Victorian era had the right idea. They wore mourning clothing to identify those who were grieving. Men wore black arm bands and widows wore special dresses for two-and-a-half years, changing the style every six months, so that the stage they were in was very obvious at a glance. Other specific garb was worn for the loss of a parent, child, or other family member and then changed at different periods of time.

My experience in the bank that day taught me two lessons that I hope I never forget. First, that grieving people are not as capable of doing tasks as they appear to be or think they are, and second, that we never know what a stranger may be struggling with in his life.

I want to remember to be gentle in my dealings with others and to not add that extra grain of sand to the mountain they may be attempting to climb. Mom and I could have used some smiles that day at the bank, and we certainly would have appreciated it if our errors had been overlooked or patiently corrected. We were functioning at our very best under the circumstances. We could also have used a friend who would have done the driving and taken over for us. We did not think we needed help and would never have asked for it. That is the reason it is so important for people to be on hand for the grieving, merely waiting willingly to assist.

5

Other Responses

W hen we are unable to get to the grieving people in person, a sympathy card with a letter or note is appreciated. A sympathy card without a letter or note leaves many people cold. It takes five minutes to write a sentence or two and it means so much more as the family rereads these messages. Poetry also seems to be very meaningful at a time of loss, and members of our bereavement-support group often share poems they received enclosed in their sympathy cards. I have seen families who have kept a box or basket filled with the special items and were still rereading them years later for comfort. Rarely have I seen a card kept and treasured that had no personal note in it.

Instead of automatically sending flowers to the funeral home, we should try to be a bit more creative. If no particular place has been designated for donations, there might be an organization that has special significance to this family. Did they work with children? How about a donation to sponsor a child at camp? Did they love to visit the forest? How about having a tree planted in a national forest? Was the death the result of cancer or heart disease? Then a donation to that research organization might be appropriate. Often trust funds are set up for the children in the family. This should be investigated. A personal touch is very meaningful at a time like this. It shows a deliberate caring and thoughtfulness, rather than automatically following the standard procedure.

Our attendance at visitations and funerals is another way of saying we care. When we attend these events, it is not for the deceased, but rather for the remaining loved ones. It is not necessary to have ever known the deceased. This is a time of coming together and participating in a formal ritual of grieving. It is a time that the remaining loved ones chose to acknowledge the closure of a life that has come to an end. Whether or not we agree with the methods chosen to express this closure is unimportant. We are not supporting the rituals or the system; we are supporting the grieving people who are left behind.

6

Anticipatory Grief

When we approach a person who is grieving, we need to be aware that the circumstances of a death can make a difference in ability to function or cope. Someone who is dealing with a sudden, unexpected death will be suffering from shock. These people will need a greater amount of assistance, tenderness, and consideration. They will hardly be able to function and they will move around as if they are in a thick fog. We must tread very carefully, to not cause them any additional pain.

When a family has been caring for a terminally ill loved one for any period of time, they are partially prepared for the death. These families have usually started to do their grief work before the death. This is called *anticipatory grief.* Funeral plans have often been discussed, and decisions may have already been made. There will be some shock to deal with; but certainly not the devastating shock that comes when a death occurs suddenly. The coping and functioning levels in these situations will also be different.

My family experienced anticipatory grief previous to my father's death. He lived for two years after he was diagnosed with cancer. He responded well to treatment, which resulted in many months of quality time as we all prepared for the inevitable. Dad spent many hours each day making lists and organizing his affairs for my mother. He talked about death, leaving no loose ends. He also spent time reaffirming his love for his family.

When his death finally came, gently and quietly, we were saddened but also relieved. We had watched his life lose all its quality and we had watched him gracefully tolerate the many indignities imposed on the terminally ill. It was time for him to move on. We knew we would miss him, but we also knew we would be reunited someday.

In our minds we had imagined the moment of my father's impending death many times. When the actual time came, we were ready to face it. My mother insisted on personally calling friends and relatives. After that task was completed, we went outside. Mom had been indoors for several months, so she welcomed the bright, sunny April afternoon. We discovered the first perky yellow daffodils of spring just peeking out of the soil and we rejoiced in the sunshine on our faces. Neighbors saw us in the yard and came over with kind words and hugs.

Everyone was prepared for this death and acceptance had begun months before. Friends, neighbors, and relatives did not hesitate to approach us. We appreciated seeing and hearing from people. I find this true in most hospice cases. Within hours, the houses are filled with people, and they remain that way until after the funeral.

The reactions were quite different from what they would have been with a sudden, shocking, or brutal death. Under those circumstances people are more hesitant to go to the survivors. Nevertheless people in shock need the support of others even more because they have not had any preparation for their loss.

7

The Shock Factor

Shock is what nature provides to allow people to carry on under unbelievable circumstances. It cushions, protects, and allows for survival when otherwise it would be impossible to function. Shock wears off slowly as the body begins to adjust to the abomination, gently easing a person toward recovery. Shock is a natural protector and should not be eased away with drugs or grabbed away by well-meaning friends. It is there to serve a purpose.

As previously mentioned, the shock factor is not as prevalent in hospice cases or with death following a lengthy illness. Sudden deaths, however, contain a startling amount of shock that can last for months. These bereaved persons will stare into space and especially do not need to be pressured into making decisions. They need the quiet strength offered from hugs, pats, and prayers.

Another difference I noticed when an unexpected death touched my life was that I experienced a wide variety of physical symptoms that I did not experience after my loved ones had died following lengthy illnesses. I had a problem with dizziness, shortness of breath, nausea, diarrhea, insomnia, and nightmares. As a result of my research, I recognized these as normal signs of shock and grief so I waited for them to disappear naturally.

Sometimes it may be necessary to call a physician to assess the situation from a medical standpoint. However, drugs should not be depended on to mask or avoid the acute pain. When drugs are used they should be only a temporary measure to ward off a specific symptom. For example, if the bereaved person seems too agitated to sleep, a mild medication may need to be prescribed for a few days. Rest is essential to face the ordeals of the following days. However, great caution should be exercised to guard against substance dependency. During intense grief it is dangerous to take hold of a crutch and end up not being able to manage without it later on. Often it is reassuring to merely be told these unpleasant physical symptoms are normal for a person who is grieving and that it is likely they will go away on their own.

Unless absolutely necessary, do not ask questions or expect immediate decisions from the bereaved. Talking seems to be especially bothersome during the period of extreme shock. Therefore it is best to try not to engage bereaved persons in lengthy conversations, but rather to allow them to sit quietly with their thoughts as they sort out their situation. When funeral arrangements have to be made, this is a large enough burden for anyone to handle. Gently advise when necessary and act as protector if anyone else is applying too much pressure for decisions. Any decisions that can be delayed should be.

During the initial shock, bereaved persons will feel very fragmented. They often cannot remember names or details. They get very easily distracted and should not be pressured into anything during this terribly stressful period. Decisions are extremely difficult to make. Their memory seems to not function. They are often irritable or even abusive to their loved ones who must be understanding about the cause behind the abuse. Forgiveness needs to flow freely during this time period.

In addition to forgiveness, endless patience is a necessity. Grieving persons will ask the same questions over and over again and then will forget the answers. They will gently need to be reminded of details. They cannot be held responsible for anything they say. They may react very defensively, and it will seem like nothing meets with their approval. These are all normal signs of grief.

8

The Forgotten Griever

Until I began to work with people who were grieving, I never thought about those who are grieving but are not considered the "next of kin." Following a death the widow or widower naturally gets an abundance of attention. But what about the possible situation where a grandchild was closer to the deceased than any other family member? This person needs special tender care but often does not receive it. We must think about this at the time of death and be sure to try and ease the grief of those who are truly the grievers and not just the next-of-kin.

A situation stands out in my mind in which a son-in-law dearly loved his father-in-law. Dave had never known his own father and his father-in-law had taken him under his wing for over twenty years. These two people had a closer, more loving relationship than many blood relatives. There were real sons in this family, too, but they had moved out of the area and were not very close to their own father. At the time of the funeral, the sons sat in the front pew at church. Dave sat off to the side.

He was not mentioned during the service when the sons were. At the conclusion, I was surprised to see Dave get up to act as pallbearer. He had been considered "just an in-law," when in fact, he was the main griever in this situation.

When a death occurs, we should think about who has been affected by this loss and let those people be the recipients of our condolences. Being remembered soothes the ache of loneliness that is left when someone we love is removed from our lives. It is especially thoughtful to send a note and sympathy card to someone whose best friend has just died. He or she is grieving and hurting and needs our thoughts and prayers every bit as much as family members.

Many times children are the forgotten ones when a death occurs. Children grieve too and they should be treated with the same respect and concern that adults receive. We assume that the young children are not capable of understanding the situation, or we may place unrealistic responsibilities on the older ones.

I know of one six-year-old boy who, when his father died many years ago was told repeatedly, "Now you are the man of the family." How ridiculous! As a result, he felt responsible whenever his mother cried following the funeral, and he certainly did not want to give up his role five years later when his mother remarried. We must be very careful of what we say to children.

Children need the opportunity to ask questions and these questions should be answered honestly. Death is a fact of life. Only when it is hidden does it become terrifying. Children should be allowed to view the body if they choose to. They can touch the body if they are curious. Of course, they should never be forced into these situations if they express fear.

When a parent dies, many times the child loses both parents—one to death and the other to mourning. Children need to be included in conversations and allowed to mourn with the remaining parent to ease the feeling of isolation or abandonment.

The main fear that children usually have when a parent dies is that something will happen to the remaining parent, and that they would be left orphans. This needs to be discussed. The remaining parent cannot promise not to die, but he or she can reassure the child of the parent's good health and the expectation to live another fifty years. The child should be told about the arrangements that have been made for him or her in the very rare event that the remaining parent does die. The children can be included in these decisions and can be present when the legal papers are drawn up. This adds a sense of security to a home that has been torn apart by a death.

When the death is that of a sibling, the surviving children fear that they, too, will die or that they are in some way responsible for the sibling's death. They must be reassured that both these ideas are not reasonable. They need to be able to discuss these fears and any others, knowing they will not be laughed at or ignored. They also need to know that life will stay as much the same as possible. The sibling can be talked about and photographs can stay on display as long as there is balance in the home so that the remaining children do not feel neglected.

The death of a grandparent is very natural and can be a time of loving reassurances and learning for a child. It is unwise to try to keep the news of a death from a child. Children have a way of knowing what is going on. Again openness is the best policy. This is a good time to share our ideas on what happens after death and to reaffirm our faith as a family.

A sensitive account of the way he handled his nine-year-old-son, Paul, following the death of his grandmother is given by Larry Richards in his book *Death and the Caring Community.*

> Late that night Paul, sleeping with me in the upstairs bedroom that had been mine as a child, began to sob. He'd been quiet and withdrawn during the last few days. He'd refused to go to the funeral home for the viewing. At the funeral he sat there motionless and just a little pale with my sister and the other relatives. Now, at last, he cried brokenly. And now, at last, I could hug him and explain that I'd brought him with me to Michigan just so he could cry. He'd been very close to his grandparents. And he needed to experience the sorrow that death brings . . . and to affirm the hope that we as Christians have.[6]

Listening to the way the child is playing with friends can be a good indicator for the feelings that he or she is experiencing. Any potential problems can be discussed at an appropriate time. Television has had a great impact on the last generation of children. They sometimes receive mistaken ideas from watching death on television. They may need to realize that in real-life people do not come alive after they have died like they do in the cartoons. Death is often viewed as being violent rather than natural and normal. All these things should be discussed with plenty of freedom allowed for questions, opinions and fears about what happens after death.

How Do We Tell The Children (Newmarket Press) is an excellent book written by Dan Schaefer and Christine Lyons. Dan Schaefer is a funeral director who has observed thousands of children. His book provides straightforward, uncomplicated answers that will help us explain the facts of death to children from toddlers to teenagers. The book includes a unique Crisis Section for quick reference during the crucial period immediately following a death. It would make an excellent book for any family where children are among the grieving.

9

Unconditional Support

Immediately after a death occurs, or while survivors are participating in the rituals of a funeral, they need our unconditional support. The course the acceptance and recovery will take depends greatly on the closure that takes place between the deceased and their loved ones. We must never stand in the way of proper closure because we feel uncomfortable or are concerned about what others might think.

A good example took place when my uncle died. It came as a tremendous shock to me. I had no opportunity to prepare for his death or to say good-bye to him. However the arrangements went smoothly until it was time for us to leave the cemetery.

We had formed a procession following the casket up a long, steep path to the gravesite. After the military ceremony was completed, we all proceeded back downhill to our cars. As we approached our car I hesitated and turned to my husband, Jack, "I just can't leave like this," I told him. He could have said, "Oh, come on. Just get into the car," or, "The ceremony is over, and we have to leave now." But he did not. Instead he thoughtfully asked, "What do you want to do?"

I was not sure exactly what I wanted to do except I knew I needed to go back up that hill. The wind was blowing, and it was bitter cold, but when I asked if we could return to the grave, he took my hand and nodded. We did not worry about the other mourners or the weather as we hiked back up the hill. The cemetery workers were ready to do their jobs but they backed away as they saw us return. I did not worry about them either. I put both my hands on the casket and had a private conversation with my precious Uncle Joe. When I had said my final good-bye, I motioned to my husband, who was standing a short distance away waiting patiently.

Jack held me close as I said one last prayer before starting down the hill again. This time I was able to breathe deeply and the heaviness that had surrounded me earlier had disappeared. Those few moments alone at the casket had given me the private closure that no other part of the formal rituals had provided. If my husband had not supported me in this need, I would have gotten in the car and left the cemetery with the agony still enveloping me. My grief would have had to slowly work its way beyond that point, instead of being released in a quick, more natural manner.

That episode helped me to understand the logic behind the claims of experts that losses need closure. Statistics show that deaths that take place as a result of war or accidents are the most difficult for people to accept. They believe this is due to the lack of closure—of not seeing the body, of not being allowed to grieve normally. Saying good-bye in a way that is comfortable to each individual is important, and we must be cautious never to take this away. Instead we can help by encouraging whatever measures are necessary for each person to perform.

I witnessed an unusual hospice case where the widow had not called our organization when her husband died in the middle of the night. Instead she had crawled into bed with him and held him in her arms until his body had lost all of its natural heat. She called us in the morning and told us what she had done. Because we are accustomed to working with death and have learned to respect each person's rights, her actions did not seem spooky or morbid to us. We understood that to her it was not a dead body she held. To her it was her loved one whose life she had shared for almost fifty years, and she wanted to keep him with her as long as she possibly could. We must all try to not judge the way people may choose to express their own grief but rather be accepting and supportive at all times.

PART 2

The Week After the Funeral

10

The Importance of Support

A week after the funeral the support that was originally sustaining the survivors decreases. Out-of-town guests will need to return home to fulfill their own responsibilities. Friends and neighbors cease to bring over food. Prayers are no longer being offered daily, and special attention is withdrawn.

Therefore this is the time for those who have taken a back-seat to come forward. Our concern, presence, and help can make a difference in the progress the bereaved person will make. "Let me know if I can do anything" is an empty offer. We need to be more specific. "How about coming over for dinner on Sunday night?" is a much better approach.

Mealtimes can be extremely difficult, and a date for any meal is a welcome change. Having breakfast with a friend can start the day off just right and gives a grieving person the incentive to get out of bed, get dressed, and leave the house. Instead of taking the bereaved person to a restaurant, an invitation to our home for a meal shared with our family is very meaningful, especially if there are children in the home. Children add a joy and lightness to life and can be a marvelous distraction.

Another thoughtful gesture is to send flowers to the home of the bereaved person with a note saying he or she is in your thoughts and prayers. One widow told us about a bouquet she received a week after her husband's funeral. It consisted of tiny pink rosebuds and dainty baby's breath, placed in a delicate glass vase with a lace edge. It made her feel pampered and loved every time she looked at it. It reminded her that she was important at a time when she was feeling insignificant, insecure, and alone.

When adult children experience the death of a parent who does not live near them, support is frequently lacking. This happens often in our transient society or with military families. The phone rings in the middle of the night with the tragic news that a parent has died. Adult children leave town to attend the funeral and are gone for about a week. When they arrive back home after this sad trip, the death seems unreal. The deceased parent did not previously have a place in their everyday life, yet a great loss has taken place.

In a case such as this, no extended family support is available, and there is usually no one to discuss the loss with or to give support to the grieving person. For these reasons, I was approached to help set up a support group at our local air force base. The support group takes the place of extended family that is not available and fills a real need for the military community.

Although I am not part of a military family, I had a similar situation when my father, who lived halfway across the country, died. I was fortunate to be able to spend the last month of his life helping to care for him and was with him at the time of his death. Five days after his death, I was back in California where the entire past month seemed unreal to me.

Waiting for me when I arrived home was a large red clay pot of spring flowers left by my close friend, Diane. I felt a surge of unexpected joy as I looked at the pansies with their little velvet faces. I had been out of town and had missed the special, short, desert springtime, but now I had these lovely little flowers to make up for it. They made me feel as if I had been missed and that my grief was shared. These were the only flowers I received, and I cherished them.

Another friend sent me notes while I was out of town. What a surprise it was to find a letter addressed to me tucked in with the usual stack of mail my parents received daily. They arrived during a time when I badly needed support, and those cards were irreplaceable.

Grieving persons whose loss drastically changes their entire lifestyle, as in the case of a child or spouse, will have a much more difficult adjustment than when an adult child loses a parent. Under those circumstances life will not just resume itself, because nothing is the same anymore. It will take considerable time for the bereaved person to reschedule his or her life. To provide help with this rescheduling, we need to listen to what the bereaved thinks are the problem areas.

The grieving person may begin expressing concerns for necessary lifestyle changes. "How will I ever manage financially?" This must never be answered lightly with platitudes. "The Lord will provide" may be a fact, but it will not bring comfort at this time. Reflective listening can be an effective response to these questions. "It sounds like you are very concerned about your finances" would be a better response. As the grieving person talks about problems, it will become easier to sort out the possible solutions.

Offers to help balance the checkbook, straighten out the paper work, or assist in obtaining phone numbers for the Social Security office are practical ways to help. The bereaved person needs to know that this problem, or any other one, will not have to be faced alone.

Psychologists have found that the number-one fear of human beings is the fear of abandonment. If we can stand nearby with our physical and emotional support and continued prayers, this fear will be lessened for the griever. Many people have told me that they can feel the withdrawal of prayers at the one-week point. Therefore it is important for us to not withdraw prayers after the funeral.

Again, as in the time of the initial contact, the mere presence of another human means a lot. It relieves the fear of abandonment just a little bit. A single white rose waiting on a colleague's desk when he or she returns to work after a death, or a short note that lets the griever know they are in our thoughts and prayers are examples of extra special ways to say, "You are not alone."

In addition to thoughtful little gifts, this is the time for walking on tiptoes. It is not the time for locker-room pep talks. Proverbs 25:20 says, "Being happy-go-lucky around a person whose heart is heavy is as bad as stealing his jacket in cold weather, or rubbing salt in his wounds." Our mood should match that of the grieving person if we wish to give support. Grieving people need to be given time to grieve. Rushing them back into a flurry of activity only prolongs or delays the grief. We would not pull a man out of bed and make him run up and down the hospital halls the day after a severe heart attack. Neither should we force a grieving person in his convalescence.

The death of a loved one is a wrenching, shocking, brutal attack on the body and like a heart attack, it requires time for proper healing. The recovery time of each person will be different, and we must adjust ourselves to their time scale.

A person's previous support system will make a big difference in the grief process. We need to assess our own support system before our lives are touched with the loss of a loved one, and make changes if we find that our entire support is held in the hands of one person. Suppose 90 percent of our support comes from our spouse. If that spouse were to die, our loss would leave us not only without our loved one, but without any support system. This may be one reason why people who have experienced anticipatory grief have an easier time dealing with grief. Their support system has changed and has been set up to effectively serve them in their time of need. We can all develop a balance in our support.

When we evaluate the support system of grieving persons, we can better understand the course of their grief work and assist them. We must never judge or compare people's grief. Instead we need to try to be understanding and come to their aid in areas where no other support is available. We also need to tread carefully as we offer assistance so that we do not add extra stress.

One woman told me that her birthday occurred a week after her husband's death. Her three children had planned a big surprise party to cheer her up. At the party they got out the old home movies, thinking this would be great fun. The woman did not consider it fun to sit and look at the happy times she had shared with her mate. To her they were knives being thrust into her heart. When she had stood all she could, she left the room in tears, much to her children's distress. It was too soon for her to take part in this frivolity. If she had been consulted, she could have chosen a more appropriate way for her family to celebrate her birthday—a way that she could handle.

Another member of our bereavement support group, Bob, told us that the day after his wife's funeral his daughter needed to return to her home in a distant state. She insisted that Bob go with her. He ended up staying many weeks, and then went on to visit other relatives who were insisting he stop by. Rushing the bereaved into frantic activities too soon is a mistake. Bob came to our group two years after the death, realizing that he had never had time to grieve previously. One of the biggest disadvantages to delayed grief is that very little support is being offered after a time lapse. The bereaved person is expected to be "over it" by this time and is not encouraged to talk about the loss.

Research has uncovered that one of the best ways to recover from grief is to talk about it. On the bulletin board over my desk is a calling card from an organization that provides grief support. It states that EVERY LOSS NEEDS ONE HUNDRED TELLINGS. I put it there to remind myself to listen. When I received that card I thought back to my own losses and roughly totaled the times I was able to "tell my story." I came up with an average of six times for each loss. It made me aware that there are few people encouraging the necessary talk about the experience of death.

11

Employers and Employees

Often the survivor returns to work after one week. I am told repeatedly that co-workers usually ignore the fact that a death has occurred. Nobody mentions it. When questioned about this omission, they respond that they did not want to make the bereaved person uncomfortable by mentioning it. However the death is the main thing on the grieving person's mind. This lack of mentioning the death makes them feel isolated and abandoned.

If the loss has been that of an elderly parent, a simple "I'm sorry to hear about your dad" can be adequate and acknowledges the loss. Even this short statement is reassuring to grieving persons. A pat on the back, a hug, or an offer to help them catch up on their work goes a long way.

If bereaved people act as if they want to pursue the conversation by beginning to talk about the deceased person or about details of the funeral, this is the time for us to stop, sit down, and practice active listening.

If the loss was more significant, such as that of a wife or child, then it will be necessary to be more understanding. Such persons may remain in shock, even after they have felt it was necessary to return to work. They may not realize the disoriented, easily distracted condition they are currently in. They will have wanted to return to work to put some semblance of order back in their lives.

If possible, we might lighten the grievers' work load or assign tasks that are easily accomplished and not critical to the company. Certainly we should mention the loss and give them the freedom to discuss it whenever possible. We can verbalize the fact that we realize they have suffered a mortal wound in their personal lives and offer assistance. We can inquire about the ways we can help both on and off the job.

In a job where grieving persons must perform at their peak for their own safety and the safety of others, the employers must take into consideration that it could take several weeks or even months for this to occur. Often the more concentration a job takes and the more involved the person can become, the easier it is to temporarily forget the grief and do the job well. If the situation looks as if it is not possible for these individuals, hopefully an alternate, temporary position could be given to such persons at this stage of their lives with the reassurances that as soon as they are ready, they can move back into their former jobs.

A small amount of extra time and caring may help the progress of working out their grief sooner and actually minimize the time and efficiency lost by valuable employees. They need to know they are secure in their jobs and not feel threatened along with all the other disruptions their lives now hold.

I was very fortunate that my losses took place while I was working for a hospice organization. Because my colleagues are familiar and comfortable with death, I received many encouraging, loving pats and I recovered very quickly. When I returned to work after my father's death, they sat me down and wanted to know all the details of his illness, the funeral, and my personal feelings. By the time I had discussed all these matters, received hugs, and shed tears with my co-workers, I felt twenty pounds lighter.

I left the office with a smile on my face. I must have received more positive strokes in one hour than most offices give in a year! Because my job is not terribly demanding, I was given as much time off, both before and after the death, as I felt I needed and I was also told to drop any activities that I felt were not healthy for me at that time. I chose to stop bereavement work for a while until I felt my own grief was worked through. How wonderful it would be if all employers had the freedom to be as generous and understanding while people are grieving. We should not have to save our grieving for after work hours.

12

Sharing Memories

The importance of providing good listening to the survivors has been previously mentioned. In addition to listening to stories about the deceased, now is the time for the sharing of memories. We need to provide extra memories for the bereaved people to take out and examine in moments of loneliness.

Barbara Bartocci in a *Reader's Digest* article says, "There are ways to fill our mental scrapbooks, of making and holding memories so we can keep those we love with us forever." She goes on to say:

> I thought about my mother's recent death. It seemed as if everywhere I went something awoke painful memories—the fragrance of her favorite perfume; a certain shade of blue; a bubbly chuckle. And yet, how lucky I was to have those memories. Painful now . . . but one day, I knew, the hurt would leave, and I would have a golden scrapbook in my mind. Through memories I could forever reclaim my mother. . . .[7]

We can help to put these golden scrapbooks together by sharing stories, letters, or photographs as soon as the survivor is able to appreciate them.

I noticed at my uncle's funeral that almost everyone explained who they were when they introduced themselves to me. "I'm Jayne. I went to school with your cousin"; or, "I'm Bill the next-door neighbor who owns the horses." Although I had not met them previously, I could connect the description to similar descriptions I had been hearing for years from my uncle and feel as if I were seeing old familiar friends.

These were the loving, caring people who had filled my uncle's life when I was unable to be with him. These were the people with whom I now shared a bond because of our common loss. It was reassuring to know I would not be the only one facing a void in my life. The ache I was feeling was being shared with me.

If these same people had been able to come forth again a week after the funeral, it would have eased my heartache a bit. I could have spent individual time with them, talking about my uncle and adding memories to my "golden scrapbook." Unfortunately, with the death of an uncle, you don't receive any sympathy cards, calls, flowers, or visitors. You can easily be the "forgotten griever." My life was expected to stay right on course with only the time taken out for the wake and actual funeral. I was given mere hours to grieve a lifelong relationship.

I realize that this was a situation where it was difficult or even impossible to make contact a week later. Our last names have never been the same. We lived almost one hundred miles apart. To be considered a griever or to be treated as one would have involved some tricky detective work. Nevertheless, how wonderful if each of us could take the time to play detective once in a while and reach out to someone who is grieving when it is least expected.

13

Decision Making

A week after the funeral some decisions may have to be made. Major decisions can still be postponed but insurance papers may need to be filed, bank accounts straightened out, or names deleted from legal documents. It is a sad fact that the bills continue to arrive and financial matters cannot be left unattended.

When a neighbor's young wife died, it was all he could do to return to his job and try to make arrangements for his children. His first major concern was to find a housekeeper so he could return to work. The neighbors gathered together and helped him find someone suitable, but we did not realize we stopped too soon with our help.

After Bill returned to work his phone was shut off. Next his trash was not picked up, and finally the water was turned off. We were afraid the housekeeper would quit! Apparently all these bills had gone unnoticed while his wife was in the hospital and remained that way after her death. It caused him extra stress and expense to have everything reconnected.

Had I realized, I could have reminded him about these items and even offered to go through the piled-up mail with him to help decide what mail needed immediate responses and what did not. A simple task like looking through the mail will seem monstrous on top of grief work. Assistance can be offered to diminish the task. Driving to the bank and standing in line with the bereaved person can ease the strain. Organizing a list of items that need to be taken care of in order of priority might be necessary.

Listening as the bereaved persons weigh the pros and cons on matters will help them to come to their own decisions. As we listen, the situation becomes clearer, and it will be easier for them to make a decision. Problems are often solved and decisions made by talking them through. Each decision that is made is a step on the road to recovery. As a friend we can offer praise and encouragement for each of these small steps.

14

The Beginning of the Grief Process

Grief can begin the first time a widow sees an envelope addressed to "Mr. and Mrs." and she realizes the "Mr." is no longer living. Or it might begin the first time a grieving mother is asked by a new acquaintance, "How many children do you have?" and she doesn't know how to answer. Grief can begin as a person goes to pick up the phone to call her dad to share a bit of exciting news, and realizes that he is no longer there to answer the phone when it rings. Grief can be finding a tiny pink stocking in the laundry basket after one's baby daughter has been a victim of SIDS. Grief shows up unexpectedly, with a jolt much like an electric shock.

In the beginning, the survivors know they have suffered the loss of a loved one but they have not as yet adjusted to a life without them. Adjusting to this new life takes time and hard work. A broken soul will mend quicker if a friend is close by acting as a crutch.

The type of friend a grieving person needs is one who does not give advice, but just stands patiently nearby watching carefully, and propping up when necessary and pitching in with practical assistance. A friend can provide a listening ear, a hug, or a reassurance that the bereaved person will survive this awful ache. True friends are those who listen with not only their ears, but with their hearts. They will listen to the complaints of every bodily ache and pain, but not encourage this talk so much that it makes it impossible to heal. A caring friend continues to offer hope when life seems hopeless.

15

The Symptoms of Grief

The symptoms of grief, as stated in my book *"When Will I Stop Hurting?"* (Baker) are *shock, sighing, crying, anger,* and *depression.* These symptoms do not occur in any certain order or last any specified amount of time. They can be passed through quickly or a person may get hung up in one stage for a long time. The stages can be repeated without any pattern. Not everyone goes through every stage, but these seem to be the most common stages experienced.

Shock

A week after the funeral the shock will still be there. The survivors will surface, look over the situation, and either continue treading water or begin to swim toward shore. The thick fog will still be surrounding them so that they cannot see the shore clearly yet.

At this time, we must let bereaved persons set the pace. We must let them suggest the tasks they wish to do. It is perfectly all right if nothing is changed yet. The grieving person may choose to wear the clothing of the deceased, sit in a favorite chair, or eat only the deceased's favorite foods. If these things bring comfort, it is not unhealthy or morbid.

I have heard some very strange-sounding stories of events that take place during this initial period of shock. We must try not to judge these actions and instead understand the reason for their occurrences. As outsiders, we need to allow grieving persons the freedom to work this loss out in their own personal way, as long as it is not causing any real harm to anyone else or to the individual. As the shock wears off, these strange actions will usually disappear automatically. Sometimes these actions will distress other family members, but that needs to be dealt with separately.

In a very rare situation there will be no shock at this time. Such was the case with Vivian, who called me the day after her husband's funeral. She wanted to join our bereavement-support group and wanted some additional information. Usually we advise people to wait about six weeks before joining. The pain is too fresh in the beginning for the wound to be touched. After six weeks the healing has begun enough that help can be given. I explained this theory to Vivian, but she insisted she was ready to attend the very next day.

It turned out that Vivian was one of those unique people who thrives on facts. She seemed to experience no shock or numbness at all. The more she knew about grief, the quicker she felt she would recover. She dug into every book on our suggested reading list and quizzed us extensively. She went and spoke to the coroner, the paramedics, and every person who had been present when her husband collapsed from a massive coronary. She carefully studied all the details and within two months was reaching out to help others who were grieving.

It would have been a mistake to slow her down. *Each person grieves differently and a helpful friend sets no limits.* They just walk along beside at whatever pace the bereaved chooses to set.

Something that should usually not be done for the griever is the clearing out or removal of the belongings of the deceased. A good portion of grief work takes place from the handling of these items. To think we are performing a good deed by removing these items is a mistake, unless the bereaved requests it specifically. It could deny bereaved persons the opportunity to experience the grief they are entitled to feel. The tears that are shed while these tasks are performed are cleansing and healing. They come from deep inside and wash away the hurt.

However, it is perfectly permissible to offer assistance in the tasks that would be too difficult to be done alone. I have stood by many a closet while the bereaved person took out articles of clothing and handed them to me. I folded the item and placed it carefully into a box.

We did this quietly, side by side, sometimes laughing over a faded, worn-out article of clothing that should have been thrown out years before—sometimes crying as we handle the favorite items that were almost like a uniform. With the transferring of each item from the closet to the box, we are removing the deceased person a tiny bit from our lives—gently, slowly, carefully, and quietly, just the way he or she should be removed.

Sighing

Listen for sighs. When people are stressed, they breathe by taking shallow breaths, depriving their bodies of oxygen. A deep sigh will increase the oxygen level and release tension.

Sighs often sound like distress signals, but they are not. They are nature's way of relieving stress by providing a soothing effect and relaxing the body. They are a good sign.

Crying

Most of us feel uncomfortable when someone cries. We are not quite sure how to act. Putting our arms around a griever and allowing him or her to cry is often all that is necessary. This may occasionally feel awkward to us, but it does not feel awkward to recipients. It allows them to be comforted. If they are never allowed the freedom to cry, they will never receive any necessary comfort.

I have the bad habit of going into the privacy of the bathroom to cry. I sob silently into a bath towel, soaking it with my tears. Then I dry my eyes, wash my face, and attack life once more. This may release the immediate stress but it certainly does not provide the loving care my family could give me if I allowed them to see me cry. I am aware that this is not a good habit and needs to be worked on.

When persons are constantly given the feeling that it is too uncomfortable for others when they cry, they will resort to the bathroom trick. Therefore we must give them permission to cry. And it is perfectly all right to cry with them. Evangelist Dwight Thompson says, "I thank God for my tears. They show I am a sensitive, feeling human being—that I'm touchable." It's good to be able to be touched by the tears of others and to let them see our tears.

At our bereavement support group meetings the very first thing we do is put a box of tissue in the center of the table. Then we tell our members that it is perfectly acceptable to cry in our presence. When someone begins to cry we try not to interfere. Usually the tears have a chain reaction, and everyone joins in. Mingled tears are one of life's blessings. They soothe and they heal. In my opinion, God uses tears to melt a heart that would otherwise stay frozen in grief.

Anger

Anger is probably the most difficult symptom to deal with both in ourselves and in others. Most of us were taught early in life that nice people do not get angry. We have spent many years learning to be "nice," even when we are not feeling very nice.

Death makes us angry. We are angry that our plans for the future are changed. We are angry at God for the dirty deal he gave us. We are angry at others who have not lost a spouse, child, or loved one. We are angry at the doctors, the mortician, the weatherman, the bank teller. In fact, we are angry at everybody and everything. Unfortunately, when this sudden anger at grief hits, nobody knows what to do with it.

When dealing with grievers, we should acknowledge that this anger is all right as long as it causes nobody harm. Do not try to talk them out of it by saying, "The doctor did his best," or "God must have had his reasons." It is better to just listen, asking creative questions that will help channel the anger along a nondestructive path.

Anger can be frightening to watch. We do not know what to do when a person seems out of control. I once watched a woman shake her fist and scream out her anger in front of our group. It scared me. However the therapist in charge just sat and listened until the woman was through. Then she told her we could all feel the anger, and it was justifiable because she had suffered a terrible blow. The therapist let her know we understood and we cared. Then she went on to suggest constructive ways to get rid of the anger through physical exercise, writing, or having a pretend conversation in private with the person she was most angry with. The main thing was that the anger was not rejected or treated as anything but normal.

Therapists have an appropriate term they use in regard to anger. It is called *venting*. I like it because I can picture a teakettle with the spout as the vent. When the water begins to boil, the steam is vented out of the spout much the way we can vent our steam as we reach the boiling point of our anger. With a teakettle we can raise the flame or lower it to control the amount of steam that will be vented. People who are grieving can be encouraged to do the very same thing with their anger. The best way to let them know they can do this is by not stopping them once they begin. If we are sensitive listeners, when the anger appears, we allow it to be vented rather than forcing it to be shut off. Shutting off the steam would cause internal pressures to build up and explode at a later date.

A good way to vent anger is through physical activity. Suggest going to an exercise class together or going on a daily morning walk. A good fast game of tennis, a bike ride, or other stimulating activity done with a friend can work miracles. We can be that friend by encouraging the activity and participating in it with the bereaved person.

Depression

Depression is a normal part of the grief process. It is the most debilitating of the stages because it comes disguised in so many varied ways. It can appear as insomnia, loss of appetite, lethargy, extreme fatigue, or a complete disinterest in life. In order to help someone who is depressed, we need to be very sensitive and gentle.

A good way to ease depression is through conversation. If grievers are allowed to verbalize their feelings, the depression can often be dispelled. In helping those who are grieving, we can encourage them to talk about their feelings and concerns.

Developing a new interest can often be constructive. A week after the funeral is too early for this, but tentative plans can be made. This will give bereaved persons something to look forward to in the future without putting stress on them to begin the activity too soon. Suggesting the bereaved enroll for a full-class schedule at the college would be unwise, but offering to take a single class with that person in a few months would be an excellent idea.

Another way to ease depression is with activity. We can offer to accompany the person who is hurting on an activity such as a walk on the beach, a hike in the serenity of the mountains, or a quiet drive in the country. Quiet activities are usually better for depression than others.

Antidepressive drugs should not be used unless the person has a history of clinical depression.

The chemical action of these medications take a long time to work and they will not relieve normal grief symptoms in a non-clinically depressed person.

Alcohol is perhaps the most common form of self-medication for the bereaved. Many sub-cultures in our society condone and encourage the use of alcohol during times of bereavement. However, because alcohol use can become psychologically as well as physically addicting, a pattern of continued use and abuse can occur.[8]

16

Physical Problems

For a grieving person, one week after the death is the point in time when physical symptoms will probably be at their worst. The distractions of company are removed, the numbness is beginning to wear off, and the shortness of breath, chest pains, or other symptoms are more noticeable. If concern over any physical symptoms is expressed, the bereaved person should see a doctor. As a friend we can offer to drive the patient to the doctor and sit with him or her in the reception room.

There is always a chance that the symptoms are the result of a genuine ailment and they should not be ignored indefinitely with the assumption that it is part of the normal grief process. When the systems of our bodies are slowed down by the grief process, illness seems to be able to take a greater hold. Colds can last for months, and stomach disorders seem to hit every day. It seems as if every germ that the bereaved person is exposed to turns into a major illness. Frequently a grieving person will require surgery. Because the healing process may be slowed down, this is a time for second and possibly third opinions before rushing into the hospital. The doctors should be alerted to the mental condition of the patient before surgery. Extra support will be required by family and friends as this takes place.

17

Guilt

Guilt can begin slinking around as soon as the fog lifts. Any statement that begins with "Why didn't I?" "I should have" or "If only" is destructive. We can remind the grieving person that the past cannot be changed. It can only be accepted. Concerns can be discussed to relieve the issue, but if the person is going around in circles, making himself feel worse, then it needs to be stopped.

Guilt can eat away and bring on physical symptoms that can be very severe. Energy will be wasted where it can do no good. Instead it could be channeled toward acceptance and adjusting to a new lifestyle. We must not discount this guilt by saying, "You have no reason to feel guilty." People cannot help the way that they feel. Instead we can let them know that we understand those feelings of guilt, that guilt is normal during grief work and that we will help them face these feelings and work them out.

A common problem among Christian grievers is that they are afraid their sorrow will make others think they have lost their faith. We must be careful to reassure them that we understand their loss is for the physical presence of their loved one that has been withdrawn. Their faith involves a divine presence and the two should not be confused. One cannot replace the other or fulfill the different areas of need. Verbalizing that we understand this confusion and clarifying that even with strong faith people grieve the death of their loved ones can ease the guilt they may be feeling. Talking about this subject can clear the air of unnecessary guilt feelings.

Again, listening is the best antidote. Also a book on grief, presented with a loving attitude, can help explain the normal grief process. It will help the bereaved person better understand the stages they are experiencing and offer solutions to the common problems faced by grieving people. (See suggested reading list.)

PART **3**

The First Six Months

18

Offering Support

T he most difficult period in recovering from a heartbreak is not the first few months. The hardest time often begins six months later when the sympathy cards stop coming. And the telephone ceases to ring," writes Robert Veninga in his book *A Gift of Hope*.

In the early weeks after a death, the grieving people are treated as if they are special. They receive extra attention and considerations. Unfortunately, this special treatment decreases just about the time the numbness and shock is wearing off, leaving the grievers very much alone. When the fog that surrounds them lifts, the void in their life becomes very visible. This happens sometime during the first six months following the death.

The encouragement of a friend during this period of time will help to fill the void. The definition of the word *encourage* is "to inspire with courage, spirit and hope." Encouragement during these months may mean listening to "tapes" being played about the deceased, even if we have heard them many times before. It will mean understanding the overwhelming lone-liness that is settling in and trying to fill some of those empty hours with our presence.

Support may need to be offered as various guilt feelings begin to surface. We can assist with the working through of those feelings by reassuring bereaved persons that they did all they could. We can use the phrase "the past cannot be changed, it can only be accepted," until it becomes a refrain they will hear whenever guilty feelings creep up. It may be necessary to offer support by gently steering bereaved persons toward re-warding activities without deterring the grief process.

The expectations of society can be unrealistic in regard to death. With careful observation and practice, we can gear our responses to the needs of each individual to provide the best support possible in each case. When we begin trying to aid someone who has suffered the loss of a loved one, we may feel awkward. Practice will build confidence and make it easier for us to do. Each person who reaches out to sustain someone who is grieving will eventually be one less person in our society who does not understand grief.

A society educated in successful grief would ease many an aching heart. Our group was made aware of the importance society plays in the grieving process by the tale of an eighty-six-year-old gentleman.

George joined our bereavement-support group shortly before the six-month anniversary of the death of his wife. He came to us very distressed because friends had been telling him he should be over the death of his wife by this time.

"We were married for sixty-four years," he told us. "Am I supposed to forget my life with her in a short six months?" He wondered what was wrong with him that he should still hurt so much and wanted us to help him "get over it."

We explained that his well-meaning friends were not being realistic. How could they possibly expect him to no longer be grieving? Society often forgets that death is the end of a life, not the end of a relationship. The memories, the love, and the time invested in that person will never disappear. We explained to George that often it makes friends uncomfortable to see someone actively grieving. They simply do not know how to deal with grief. We then told him that he could cry and talk about his wife as much as he needed to when he was with us. It would not make us uncomfortable and it would certainly help him in working through his grief.

He did just that. He cried copious tears that he had been holding back for the sake of others. And as a result of his participation in our group, he made a whole new circle of friends. All these friends were also grieving and understood his situation. In each other they found the understanding and support that was lacking from their relatives and friends who did not understand grief and its process. The group would go out for lunch or play a game of cards. When someone was having a bad day, he or she would call another member and ask for help.

Grief does not automatically disappear with time. E. M. Blaiklock has been quoted as saying, "Time does not heal. The task is one of courage, faith, the will to conquer. It is like the task of the disabled, the halt, the lame, the blind. There is no healing, only victory to pursue, and the twisting of disaster into something God can use for others."

Grief is work—hard work. It has to be talked out, cried out, acted out, before changes can be made. This process takes time and that is the reason society assumes that time heals the hurt. In actuality, it is the work taking place during the passage of time that is easing the pain. The lost loved one is never forgotten; the pain never disappears. However, as the grieving person adjusts to a new lifestyle acceptance arrives. With acceptance, the agony eases gradually until at last it is hardly noticed. We have seen people five years after the death of a loved one who are in acute, active grief. They were just beginning to face the loss and work it out after all that time. Time did not make it go away at all. It still had to be worked through.

19

Listening Skills

It has been established through studies that one of the best ways to work through grief is by talking about it. Therefore, grieving people are going to need their friends to listen as they talk away their grief. I was once told that the reason I have two ears and one mouth is because I am to listen twice as much as I talk. Good advice, but not very easy to follow. Being a good listener does not come naturally to most people. It is a skill that is learned from constant practice. Anyone who wants to be able to help a person who is hurting needs to learn active, sensitive, and reflective listening skills.

Active listening is a communication technique that avoids the interference of a listener's judgment. It is the understanding of what is being said without imposing our own judgments, advice, or analysis on the speaker. It is a highly effective tool in situations where we want and need to understand what we are being told. It also has the added advantage of being a useful device for helping others clarify their feelings.

Reflective listening goes a step further with the listener paraphrasing or "reflecting" back the statement to assure the speaker that he or she has been heard. For example, the speaker might say, "I'm too tired to even think straight." This is paraphrased back by the listener as, "It sounds to me as though you are feeling overwhelmed and exhausted." Another example, "I don't know what to do. There are too many decisions to make." This can be paraphrased as, "You must be feeling quite pressured over all this new responsibility."

This is not merely parroting the speaker. If we echo the speaker before allowing the conversation to continue, it lets the person know we have heard what was said. It allows the grievers to form their next thought without the thought process being interrupted. It also provides us with necessary information to enable us to best assist the grieving person.

Active listening encourages the speaker to expand on the problem by responding with a statement such as, "Yes, go on," or "Tell me more about that."

If the person has trouble clarifying his or her thoughts, we can respond with, "Then this is the problem as you see it," and repeating back the information, again using paraphrases. If we are incorrect in our assumptions, the speaker can correct us, which will also clarify the griever's thoughts.

Both *active and reflective listening* also involve hearing the tone of voice the speaker is using. "I can hear that this situation makes you angry," or "You must be feeling very helpless about this problem." These statements allow the speaker to expand the idea and hopefully to find a possible solution without us having to give advice. *Giving advice is generally not helpful to a person who is agonizing over a situation.*

Death and the Caring Community uses the term *sensitive listening*. Sensitive listening involves our full attention.

There are a number of ways to let a person know we're giving him or her our full attention. We sit down in the room rather than remain standing. We draw up our chair closer rather than keep space between us. We maintain good eye contact . . . and nod in response to his words. Each of these very simple things says loudly that the other person is important; that we are concentrating our attention on him rather than ourselves . . .

Listening sensitively means focusing on the thoughts and feelings expressed by the individual, and being willing to respond to them. It involves more than discerning how an individual feels. It involves responding in an acceptable or supportive way.[9]

When we avoid eye contact, fold our arms, or lean away from a person, we are using body language that comes across as the wish to withdraw from the speaker. Instead, we need to reflect back feelings in some simple way that lets the person know we have heard and understood what was said. Paraphrasing is one technique; good body language is another.

Active listening keeps the door open to further sharing. It helps the individual express feelings and put experience into words. If we show shock, act judgmental, condemn, or give advice, it can stifle any further sharing. It is better to show loving acceptance, letting others know we are there in a supportive manner.

While listening to someone, it is important to touch the person at the proper times. Grabbing a hand, patting or putting an arm around someone as they try to say something touching or difficult gives them the courage to express themselves more fully. They physically feel the support. Likewise, asking questions indicates interest and shows caring.

I had an acquaintance of over twenty years who I never felt cared about me. For many years I was uncomfortable in this person's presence until one day I came to the realization that it was because I felt a lack of interest on her part. As I prayed and thought about the situation, I understood that it was because she never asked any questions. She never asked, "What have you been doing lately?" She never asked, "Do you have any special projects going?" and she never, ever asked about my writing. All these things hurt me, and I often wondered why, after so many years, she took no interest in me.

After further prayer, I came to the realization that it was not a lack of concern, interest, or caring. Rather, it was the result of a strict upbringing that considered the asking of questions to be rude or prying. I began to experiment by asking the questions myself.

"Would you like to see the dresses I'm sewing for the girls?" I would ask. She always responded enthusiastically. It took a lot of practice on my part before I was comfortable doing this but it brought about a very beautiful relationship that never could have developed otherwise.

I once heard someone say, "Questions are like the banks of a river; they channel the flow of the conversation." When we ask questions, it bridges the gaps in conversation. It shows we care. The questions should not be invasive or rude, of course, but ones that show we are truly interested in the things that matter to the other person.

Creative, sensitive listening interspersed with questions can be the most helpful tool we have to offer people who are grieving. It allows them the opportunity to vent their anger and confusion. It allows them to begin to form plans for the future. It expels the feelings of aloneness or abandonment as it comforts, giving the reassurance that someone does care.

20

The Death of a Parent

It has been brought to my attention in confidential conversations with relatives, friends, and acquaintances that six months after a spouse has suffered the loss of a parent is a critical point in a marriage.

I believe it may be because in the early months after the loss, the spouse is understanding and supportive of the griever. After six months have passed, the griever is still seeking nurturing from their spouse, who is also grieving and does not have a plentiful supply of sympathy to give out. This can cause bad feelings between the couple as irritability and tension build up.

If the person whose parent has died is experiencing guilt over the neglect of this parent, it will add to the problem. If the spouse did not get along with the in-law, that adds extra stress. If a lengthy illness prior to the death disrupted the family, extra adjusting will be involved. There may have been financial problems brought on by huge medical bills. So many factors go into each, and every relationship that it is too complex to draw any concrete conclusions, but any of these situations can be explosive.

There is no easy answer to ironing out the wrinkles in a marriage except that under these circumstances, time does have a way of helping. If we are the spouse of a person who is grieving, we need to realize that six months is a short period of time in regard to grief. We will need to extend our love and compassion a bit longer. We would not purposely want to add to the anguish of our spouse. Encouraging our grieving partner to talk about pleasant memories of childhood might help open the doors that will permit guilt and anger to escape. This is an especially important time to be a good listener.

As difficult as it might seem at times, we can try to be loving, comforting, and understanding to our grieving spouse. We need not feel pressured to retaliate when we feel we have been wronged. And we need to spend as much time as possible in prayer.

When a person is at his or her least lovable is the time when he or she needs love the most. Of course, that is the time when it is hardest to be loving toward that person. First Corinthians 13:4–7 tells us,

> Love is very patient and kind, never jealous or envious, never boastful or proud, never haughty or selfish or rude. Love does not demand its own way. It is not irritable or touchy. It does not hold grudges and will hardly even notice when others do it wrong. It is never glad about injustice, but rejoices whenever truth wins out. If you love someone, be loyal to him no matter what the cost. You will always believe in him, always expect the best of him and always stand your ground in defending him.

It is wise to be aware that the six-month point can be a difficult time. It gives us something to be wary of. By simply watching for problems, they can sometimes be averted before they get serious. Understanding the basis of the winter season can make it easier to await the springtime.

21

Disposing of Belongings

Our hospice team has a rule of thumb that we follow in regard to the disposing of personal belongings and clothing of the deceased. We feel that the task should be begun during the first six months after the death or it is a sign of a potential problem.

This does not mean there cannot be a single item in the house that belonged to the deceased. It means that some thought, decisions, and disposal of clothing and personal items should have taken place. It means that tools that will never be utilized again should be given away. If there is a car, camper, truck, or boat that is no longer needed, it should be put up for sale or given away. The slippers of the deceased should no longer be under the dining room table or the coat hung over the back of the hall chair. To have items like this around indicates that the griever is still expecting the deceased to return. If proper grief work has taken place, the person has by this time accepted the fact that the loved one will not be returning home again. As a caring presence, if we see these disheartening signs, we can offer assistance in clearing out a closet. Often the grieving person has not begun the task because he or she has no incentive. We can give the incentive by suggesting a needy person or organization who would put the articles to good use. If we offer to help with the task, it will make it easier to begin. We can even be the one who physically removes the articles from the household as long as the grieving person has taken part in the sorting. (This was discussed in further detail in chapter 15 under Shock.)

Photographs, souvenirs, memorabilia, and even some clothing can certainly be kept. In fact, putting old photographs in albums can be a task that is very rewarding at this time. It recalls happy memories and rids the mind of the torment associated with a terminal illness or funeral that might otherwise be the only recent memories.

22

Loneliness

As mentioned previously, loneliness is very prevalent during the first six months. A caring friend will spend time with the bereaved person and will include him or her in their family's activities. However, we must not be persistent if the bereaved refuses an invitation. Once an invitation has been extended, we must not feel hurt if it is turned down. Likewise, we should not withhold future invitations because of the refusal. At various times, grieving people feel differently about what they can participate in.

We advise our bereavement-support group members to assess invitations carefully before accepting them. We suggest they merely ask, "Can I get back to you on this?" They should picture themselves in the situation and decide whether or not it would be healthy for them. If they feel the situation would be too uncomfortable, they must express this and refuse the invitation.

Betty told us that after her husband died, friends invited her to go to his company picnic with them. She felt uncomfortable about it and declined. The friends insisted she had always attended the picnic and needed to go "for her own good."

She felt very hesitant, knowing it would stir up memories of all the company picnics she and her husband had attended together. She would be seeing her husband's colleagues that she had not seen since his funeral. The more she thought about it, the less she felt she should attend.

The morning of the picnic, her friends arrived at her house and almost dragged her with them. They refused to listen to her explanation and even told her they had packed extra food especially for her. At last she decided she had no choice but to join them. It was the worst day she had had since her husband died.

She cried and cried as she tried to tell us about it. Her sixth sense had told her she should not go, but it took too much energy to be assertive against such strong competition. The friend of someone who is grieving must remember to be sensitive to that person's needs instead of one's own ideas of what would be "good for them."

That same day we heard an unbelievably beautiful story from Ann, who had been on vacation for a month. Prior to his death, Ann's husband and she had been planning a month-long camping trip with very dear friends. Two months before the trip, Ann's husband had suffered a fatal heart attack. Ann decided to make the trip anyway. Everyone in our group felt it would be a mistake, and that she would be miserable visiting all the places she and her husband had mapped out together. But Ann had weighed all the possibilities and decided this trip should be made. We waited for her return with bated breath.

When she returned, with smiles, she reported that it had been a wonderful vacation. "Jim would have wanted me to go," she told us. But the best part had been the friends. They apparently were very special, sensitive people. They had talked frequently about Jim and had cried openly over their loss. As they shared golden memories, past and present, it had been almost as if Jim was on the trip with them. All this had been thoroughly therapeutic for Ann. She came home rested, relaxed, and refreshed. Apparently, she had known what was the wisest choice and had taken it.

Widows and widowers claim that dinnertime is the worst time of the day. As families gather together at the end of the day, the emptiness of their own home is jarring. They claim it is terribly depressing to prepare a meal for themselves and eat alone. Dinner invitations seem to be greatly appreciated but are rarely extended.

Widowers frequently have a problem with cooking. We might be able to offer them some cooking hints, a very simple cookbook or assistance in basic cooking skills.

When I took a microwave-cooking class several years ago, I observed a daughter attending the class with her widowed father. They were both learning a method of cooking that would make meal preparation more simple. It was delightful to watch them together, as she provided the opportunity for him to become more independent in his new life.

I am told that Sunday seems to be the longest day in the week for people living alone. We advise our bereavement-support group members to plan in advance for times that are the most difficult by setting up a luncheon date following church or making plans for a Sunday-afternoon outing. Those of us who are not alone might want to look around our church to discover who is returning to an empty house and ask them to join our family for brunch. Often during the grief process it takes too much energy for the grieving person to reach out and mingle, so we need to extend our hands first.

In our desire to ease loneliness for grieving people, we might keep several things in mind. Each situation is different and must be evaluated before acting in a way that might add to the burdens the grieving person is already carrying. We must respect their decisions and not be too forceful when an invitation is declined. And we can keep in mind that frequent cards, notes, and phone calls, all let the person know they have not been forgotten.

23

Forgiveness

Unforgiveness that is being nurtured inside a grieving person can add to feelings of loneliness. Granted, it is not for us to judge, but if we see our grieving friend clutching tightly to angry feelings and unforgiveness, we can try to cautiously ease this pain by suggesting prayer for forgiveness over the specific situation. When we originally approach this subject, we may be met with defensiveness and even more anger. However the first seed has been sown. As time goes on that seed can be watered with careful suggestions that will promote more thought along the lines of forgiveness.

I have personally found that each suggestion I make is met with less resistance until finally the unforgiving persons reach the point where they think the idea of forgiveness originated within themselves. Occasionally, a mere suggestion is adequate, and they will eagerly approach the subject of forgiveness themselves. I have seen many examples of forgiveness versus unforgiveness, and it never ceases to amaze me how different the effect is on the grieving person.

It takes a vast amount of prayer to bring about forgiveness toward a person who has mortally wronged us. To forgive the drunk driver who killed their only child, a seven-year-old-tow-headed lively boy, or the son-in-law, who brutally murdered their twenty-year-old pregnant daughter is a feat possible only with the help of God. As friends of these grieving people, we must tread carefully while offering up prayer for the words we might use in regard to forgiveness.

When their only son was killed while riding his motorcycle, Lynn and Bob were naturally devastated. A week later they began to think about the young man who had been driving the automobile that had hit their son. He had not been at fault, no drugs or alcohol had been involved. It had been late at night with poor visibility when the motorcycle rider had pulled out in front of the car. Tire marks showed he had swerved to avoid the accident, but it had not been possible.

Bob told me, "One life was taken. We could not let this accident ruin another life. So we contacted the automobile driver and invited him to meet with us. We assured him that we did not blame him and that we wanted to help him forgive himself."

They had all three cried together over what seemed like such a sudden, meaningless loss. All three lives had been drastically changed in the split second it took for the accident to occur. But now all three people wanted to work together to ease each other's pain. They have kept in touch since the accident, filling a need in each other's lives as healing slowly takes place.

With forgiveness comes an inner peace—an acceptance of what cannot be changed—a starting point for healing. With unforgiveness comes more distress, an inner festering of an unclean wound, and a roadblock to progress. No joy can flow through this roadblock.

24

Holidays

Another time when loneliness takes hold is when holidays approach. They bring about an extra feeling of isolation for the grieving people. In fact, holidays seem to be the largest obstacles in the path to recovery. For weeks in advance the stores display cards, gifts, and signs making it impossible for a grieving person to shut out the fact that this is the first Father's Day to be faced without a father to phone, the first Christmas without that special person to shop for, or the first Valentine's Day without a sweetheart.

Old traditions are destroyed and new ones do not fit properly. Dorothy told us that the Christmas after her son died she was invited to her cousin's house for the holiday season. He lived in a distant state and thought a change of scene would be good for her. She had refused at first, but he had insisted she not spend the holidays alone. She boarded the plane apprehensively.

She said she had felt uncomfortable the entire week, pretending to be having a good time. She knew her relatives meant well and she did not want to ruin the holiday for anyone else, so she tried to put up a good front. It took tremendous effort.

The following year when she was invited back, she gently explained that she planned to stay at home alone for the holidays. She was grateful for the invitation but was even more grateful when her cousin said he understood. She was given the freedom to choose the way she would spend her day without being made to feel guilty. She confided in us that she would be happier alone with a good book and a frozen dinner than having to wear a facade.

A phone call, note, card, or meal invitation on any holiday, even insignificant ones, will be greatly appreciated. Personal holidays such as the birthday of the deceased, the birthday of the grieving person, anniversaries, or any other day that was special, are made a little easier if they are shared with or remembered by an encouraging friend.

Remembering that it has been six months since the death with a phone call or card sent to arrive on that date will also be appreciated. Grieving people are very aware of significant dates.

I called my mom on my dad's birthday the first year after he had died. I had not planned to mention the date unless she mentioned it first, but I wanted to talk to her that day. She answered the phone and as soon as she heard my voice, inquired, "Do you know what today is?" Seldom does the grieving person forget. But Mom had very cleverly set up a luncheon date with several lady friends and planned to have dinner with my sister. "I'm not just going to sit home and feel gloomy today," she informed me. Good for her!

We can help our friends get through these days by making ourselves available if they happen to issue an invitation.

25

Toughlove

*T*oughlove is a term usually associated with parenting. It can also apply to someone who is grieving. The six-month anniversary can be a time when it may be necessary to apply toughlove.

As a caring friend we will want to be understanding and supportive of the grieving person. However, there are rare exceptions, when the grieving person is being manipulative and must be dealt with in a different manner if any progress is to take place.

I saw a good example of this in Richard, who is a strong, healthy seventy-year-old man. He spent several years caring for his terminally ill wife before her death. When she died, he was left with no remnants of a life of his own. He would pace and wring his hands while big tears ran down his cheeks. Friends and neighbors rallied forth following his wife's death. They drove him shopping, cleaned his house, and invited him over for dinner. They almost smothered him with attention because he looked so pathetic.

After a few months of this tender, loving care, they gradually withdrew some of their support because Richard had appeared to be doing quite well. He was attending our bereavement-support group, was learning to cook and was even planting a garden. Then, all of a sudden, he regressed back to the crying, wringing of the hands, and refusing to attend our group. He would complain that it was too depressing to eat alone and stopped eating entirely. He even threatened suicide.

Immediately his friends and neighbors came forward. They took his hand and led him over to their homes for dinner. Again Richard thrived until the support lessened. This happened several times until the friends and neighbors became weary and called us for advice.

Our consulting therapist explained that they were reinforcing Richard's negative behavior so that he found it more productive to not recover from his grief. A pattern was developing that needed to be broken. Of course, nobody wanted to be cruel and reject his calls for help. First, they had to be sure that he was not truly needy. This was confirmed by our therapist who observed that when Richard was getting his own way, he was cheerful and happy. When left to his own resources, he reverted back to crying, refusing to eat, and literally wringing his hands. We were told this was the time for "toughlove."

Toughlove was shown by giving Richard praise and support for anything constructive that he accomplished instead of only coming to his aid when he was depressed. This was very difficult to stick to and many times there was failure. However eventually the special treatment paid off, and Richard was able to drive himself to the store, invite friends to his house for dinner, and feel more positive about his life. At the same time he was working through his grief instead of just manipulating people who would be distractions to the acceptance of his new lifestyle.

If we see a negative pattern forming, we should suggest professional help. We can offer to do the telephoning to set up the appointment and even provide transportation. We might also want to seek professional advice on how to deal with this person to assist in the recovery.

26

Bereavement-Support Groups

Making the decision and attending a bereavement-support group may be too difficult for grieving persons to do on their own. Bereavement-support groups are advertised in the newspaper, sponsored by hospitals or hospice organizations. Making inquiries about the group and offering to attend with the bereaved person for the first time or two is a very thoughtful gesture. Many of our members were brought to our group for the first time by someone who had attended the group previously or by a hospice volunteer.

Group situations are not for everyone but it is always worth a try. I am continually amazed at how fast grieving people progress in a nurturing, compassionate atmosphere. It warms my heart to see the caring that goes on between our members. No matter how intense their own pain, most people will reach out and put their arm around the person sitting next to them to provide comfort. As they look away from their own pain, it begins to diminish.

When I look around these groups, I see many biblical teachings at work. Feelings seem to be so close to the surface in grieving people that they truly "do unto others as you wish they would do unto you."

PART 4

The One-Year Anniversary

27

A New Lifestyle

A long year has passed since my husband died. I have tried to put into perspective some of the emotions suffered, stages of grief, and steps of recovery as I have had to adjust to a new life. They say time heals all wounds. It still has work to do. Knowing that there is a merciful God who understands and cares, a loving family and many dear friends to help bear the sorrow served to sustain me when I felt utterly cast down.[10]

The one-year anniversary date of the death is a milestone. Each holiday, birthday, and anniversary has been endured during that year. The income tax form, bank statements, and finances have been dealt with. The oil in the car has been changed, the Christmas tree lights have been figured out, and the buttons have been sewn on the jacket. In other words, a new lifestyle, filled with many changes, has been adopted.

Bereaved persons will still have an empty place in their hearts and lives, but hopefully some positive changes and adjustments will accompany the emptiness. As caring friends, this is the goal we will have been encouraging all year long.

When I asked grieving people to tell me what they appreciated most at the end of the first year, they listed three things:

1. assistance in practical matters
2. having their loved one remembered
3. the physical presence of caring friends or family

I was told that the assistance in practical matters that was offered immediately following the death ceased by the one-year mark. Nevertheless this was the time when that help would be greatly appreciated. Many items need to be repaired and practical tasks need to be figured out for the first time. A simple chore like changing a light bulb can seem overwhelming to a person who is grieving. Many widows told me people offered their help but never followed through. These empty offers seemed to hurt more than no offers at all.

An example of a positive way to give assistance was told to me by a widow. She told me that the day after Christmas a young couple from her church appeared at her door. The man said, "I got a new saw for Christmas. Is it okay if I try it on that wood you have out back?" While he cut the wood, his wife sat in the kitchen and visited. After they had finished and gone, the widow looked outside and to her amazement every log had been cut into small, handy pieces, just the right size for her.

Her eyes filled with tears as she shared this story. "I appreciated the kind way in which that help was offered. It didn't make me feel needy or inadequate. The young man almost made it sound like I was doing him a favor by letting him cut my wood with his new saw." A thoughtful task of this type appears to be the most appreciated.

Remembering to mention the loved one is especially important, even after a year. So often grieving people feel nobody remembers this special person, misses them, or cares about them any longer. One woman said she was especially touched by her pastor, who as he struggled with the movie projector, muttered, "Where's Ray when I need him?" She said her husband had always been the church member who came to the rescue when they had mechanical problems, and she was delighted to know he had been appreciated and was missed.

Letters are wonderful ways of uplifting a grieving person. Almost a year after my father died, I received a letter from a friend of his. I had never met the man, but I had heard Dad speak of him often. He wrote that he could picture my dad in heaven organizing committees to accomplish great feats (this made me smile because Dad had truly been a great organizer). He wrote several other clever anecdotes, including the fact that now everything in heaven was probably having to be done in triplicate (Dad thought if one of something was good, three were better!), and closed by telling me that I had inherited my writing ability from my dad, and that he lives on in everything that I write. I had not thought about that previously. I have two daughters who write also, which means that Dad left a legacy for at least two more generations, with the possibility of many more to come. I am uplifted by the knowledge of this inheritance.

That letter may have taken an hour to write, but I will cherish it for the rest of my life. It contained not just meaningless sentimentality, it contained personal comments that brought Dad back to me for a little while, and made me smile over the endearing personality traits that were so unique to him.

On the actual date of death, one year later, the grieving person relives all the events that took place the previous year. At noon they will remember they were dressing for the funeral service. At three o'clock they were standing by the graveside.

Even if they were in a state of complete shock, they still seem capable of bringing those emotions up to the surface again, experiencing the intense anguish they felt the previous year.

Having the physical presence of someone who cares, sharing the actual anniversary date, is very important. Possibly a sympathetic friend could suggest an activity for this date that would commemorate the sad occasion in a suitable manner. Possible appropriate activities might be having family members attend a church service together, and then share a meal, or gathering friends and family to plant a tree or flowers at the gravesite. Jewish tradition gathers loved ones together to go to the cemetery for the placing of the headstone on the one-year anniversary date. In this way loving support is available when it is most needed.

If it is not possible to be physically present with the grieving person, a single rose delivered to the home of the bereaved or flowers given to the church in remembrance can bring great comfort. Remembering the favorite flowers of the deceased, or a favorite recipe, and sharing it with the grieving family is another means of commemoration. Any action that lets the grieving person know that they are not suffering alone, that there are other people who care and who are also missing their loved one, is meaningful.

28

Change in Residence

ften people are thinking about or getting ready to change their place of residence by the one-year anniversary date. Frequently this is done from a financial standpoint. Widows may prefer condominiums or apartments, where the maintenance is done for them. Mobile homes are also popular. They seem to be safer for elderly people living alone and offer an opportunity to become part of a small community.

People living in the country may wish to move into town for safety and convenience. They have had a year to think about the move and can choose wisely at this point. Moving before the year is up is usually discouraged. When acute grief work is going on, it is too difficult to make wise decisions.

If the move is decided on after a year, we can help a friend move and enthusiastically assist. Putting in kitchen shelfpaper together is much more fun than doing it alone. Choosing carpet or wallpaper often requires a second opinion. We can stand by the grieving person's side and make a change in residence easier and more fun. The move may also precipitate the final cleaning out of the garage or closets and disposing of the remnants of the lost loved one's belongings. This chore is easier, too, when shared.

With a change in residence, many unhappy memories can be put aside. A home holds so many memories, both good and bad. Frequently a fresh start can begin only in a new home. We no longer have that special bedroom that belonged to the deceased or the room our loved one may have died in. We won't have the garden that we planted together or the home that held so many plans for the future that became lost dreams after the death. We can leave behind the prospective nursery that would continue to be a reminder as long as it remained empty.

If a grieving person is talking about a change, it should be encouraged but seldom forced. To uproot a widow, talk her into selling the home she has been in for thirty years, and move her in with another relative is not usually a good choice. Deep thought and much discussion should occur while the positive and negative aspects are carefully examined. The final choice must be that of the bereaved person and not necessarily the easiest solution for another family member.

According to medical experts, any change to new living quarters is traumatic and very often results in illness. This is true even when the move is eagerly anticipated. Some caregiver should be responsible to keep a sharp eye on the newly relocated person and watch for such illnesses.

Dot and her mother are typical examples of a story I hear frequently. Dot was an only child. When her father died, she insisted her mother sell her house on the East Coast and move in with her. She reasoned that the California climate would be easier for her mother to cope with than the severe eastern winters. She had an extra bedroom and she and her husband were eager for Mama to be with them. They would no longer have to worry about her living alone, so far away. They helped her sell her home and all the furnishings.

However, Mama was not happy in California. She missed her senior citizen's group and her church work. She missed having her own home and garden to putter around in. She felt like a perennial guest who did not belong. Dot finally had to move her into her own apartment back east, but of course they could never replace all the belongings she had parted with. We must be very careful, especially in transplanting elderly people.

Contrary to this unfortunate situation was Gail, who after considerable deliberation sold her home and moved into a condominium. I visited her on the year anniversary date of her husband Bob's death. I was eager to see how she was adjusting. On entering her new home, I was startled to see an entirely new look about it. She had changed her accent color to a dusty mauve. It looked lovely.

She laughed when I remarked on it. "I have always loved mauve," she told me, "but Bob hated it. It dawned on me just before I moved that *now* I could have all the mauve I wanted in my new home!" She went on to tell me, in a whisper, that she had even treated herself to a new negligee set in matching mauve. I was so pleased to see Gail actually joking about this. It showed tremendous progress in the acceptance of a new lifestyle. She had found some advantages to living alone and was concentrating on the positive aspects rather than the negative ones.

29

Other Changes

s is true in regard to changes in residence, changes in traditions will have been necessary during the first year. If these changes worked out successfully, they can become the new traditions. If they were unsuccessful, more experimentation will have to take place until a satisfactory solution is reached. A supportive friend can help with these decisions. Being a sounding board is important as the grieving person tries to make changes.

Advice is not necessary. Merely listening as the person comes to his or her own conclusions is more helpful. Again we can apply our sensitive and reflective listening skills as ideas are forming and decisions are being made.

Positive changes are to be applauded. They reinforce the desire to reestablish a meaningful existence. Frequent experimentation may be necessary before the new lifestyle is established.

Women often begin their acceptance and adjustment process with outward signs of changes in their appearance such as a new outfit, a new hairstyle or a new hair color. We can gently suggest these changes by offering to join in a visit to the beauty shop or a shopping trip to a city mall to choose some new clothes. It is always easier to do these things in the company of a friend.

Men often grow beards, mustaches, or buy a new car as they venture into their new life. They may appreciate help in practical matters such as cooking and doing the laundry, rather than in experimenting with their physical appearance. Many men dislike shopping for clothing, so we might like to purchase a new flannel shirt to lift such a person's mood. Each person is different, but by listening we will be able to ascertain the best way we can help in this individual's healing process even after a year.

Parents who have suffered the loss of a child very often wish to work with children to fill the void. One young mother started a day-care center so she could fill her arms with cuddly babies and her ears with the sound of children's laughter. A father volunteered for the Big Brother program and spent his empty Saturday afternoons throwing a softball to a fatherless boy. As each one reached out, his own pain lessened.

30

Reaching Out

Often it is too difficult to do the reaching out alone. This is where a friend can assist. We can look for areas that would be interesting to the bereaved person and then offer to join in these activities. If physical exercise is an area that appeals to this particular person, we can suggest taking an aerobics class together, obtain the information, and jointly register for the class.

If learning a new skill is the area to be pursued, we can make some phone calls and have a list of available choices in our community, and volunteer to participate in the activity with our grieving friend. This skill can be something creative like a ceramics class, a tole painting class, or a college course on skills such as a class on investments or simple car maintenance.

Volunteers are becoming scarce. As a result, most organizations, churches, groups, and communities have great unfulfilled needs. A few phone calls can be made to establish a list of available places where help is needed.

If structured, scheduled activities seem to be unappealing to the grieving person, it may be more helpful for us to be on hand for an occasional game of tennis, a walk in the park, or a luncheon date instead. Whatever activity is appropriate, it will be easier when not done by oneself.

As a caring friend, we can encourage grieving persons to reach out to others who share the same grief they have experienced. The kindred spirit between two mothers suffering the loss of a child, or two widows helping each other can be a soothing balm to the wound. ". . . seasons for tears teach us how to begin to sympathize when others cry . . . How comforting are those rare ones who sense our frightened, darting eyes and move right in with precisioned, knowing comfort. Many times they do so in silence, leaving chatter to less trained—the ones with all the answers," writes J. Grant Swank, Jr.[11] This is one of the reasons that bereavement-support groups are so successful. The understanding that flows between similar suffering can entwine to reinforce unraveled lives.

This does not mean the bereaved should burden a newly grieving person with their own tales of grief. It means they can put the anguish of their own losses to good. In using the empathy, sensitivity, and understanding they wished others had used with them, they can serve a great need. At the same time that they are reaching out they are hastening their own recovery.

Susan told me she had many visitors following the death of her husband. She appreciated them all, but she admitted the most comfort came from Marlene, who had been widowed two years before. She said, "Marlene knew all the right things to tell me. She told me to go ahead and cry and that my pain was understandable." She had not told her to "cheer up" or that "time would make everything better."

Susan could look at Marlene and see her healthy glow. She could see her smile as they held hands. She could see living evidence that a widow had recovered and it offered hope that she, too, would recover someday.

31

Delayed or Displaced Grief

U p to this point, we have been discussing normal grief. Occasionally we will come on a situation that does not fit the norm. A person who was unable to grieve at the time of the death may show signs of extreme grief at a much later date. This is not a matter to be concerned about. Grief worked out at anytime is better than grief left unresolved. I have seen several classic cases of delayed grief.

One came about as a result of Bob's relatives keeping him overly busy traveling and visiting immediately following his wife's death. He came to us experiencing delayed grief. When he had returned home after his travels many months later, the empty house hit him with a force that almost destroyed him.

While Bob had been traveling, he had not faced the reality of his wife's absence. He could still picture her at the kitchen sink and sitting in her favorite chair in front of the television set. When he arrived home, he was forced to face the fact that she no longer physically shared his life. Her clothes were still hanging in the closet, her toothbrush was in the bathroom, but she was no longer there.

As he reached out looking for support, he could not find any. Friends and neighbors had thought by this time "he would be over it." No meals were brought over. No offers to accompany him to the bank were forthcoming. He was on his own—all alone. Fortunately, he found his way to our bereavement-support group, and the other members reached out to help him begin his walk along the path of recovery. They allowed him his season of tears that would eventually produce a crop of sensitivity and caring for others.

If we see a situation of delayed grief, we must immediately try to help with our presence and the tasks we ordinarily would have done right after the death occurred. We might also be able to enlist the aid of others who may not realize a delayed need has arisen.

The other case I saw involved a mother whose twelve-year-old son had been killed in an accident. The mother had been studying to become a registered nurse. She continued to attend classes and amazed everyone with her capacity to function. After graduation she began work at a local hospital. She came to see us because she was being transferred to the pediatric-oncology ward and realized she could not face working with children.

She was at last facing her unresolved grief and knew it had to be dealt with before she could function properly. She took a three-month leave of absence from work, attended our group, went into private therapy, and finally cleared out her son's belongings. In the beginning we observed that she could not sit still in her chair. I have never seen a person in such constant motion. She twisted, turned, swung her foot. She was a tightly strung top, just waiting to spin out of control. When she spoke, her words came out fast and furious. When she cried, she sobbed from the depths of her very soul.

Six months later, I was pleased to see the success of her various treatments. She sat calmly with a smile on her face. She shared with us the anguish and despair she had experienced in those six months. She had worked hard to overcome her grief, but she reassured us that it had been well worth the work and pain. She was again looking forward to her new career and felt an inner strength and peace she had not had in her life previously. She was making plans to work with the parents of her pediatric patients to help them understand the care of terminally ill youngsters. She hoped to use the death of her son to develop her own inner strength that would enable her to help others.

Delayed grief can be more visible and intense than normal grief. It is more difficult to deal with but very necessary. It is an area that we can watch for when we see normal grief being bypassed. Eventually it is going to erupt and need the help of a caring friend or relative if it is going to be worked through.

Displaced grief is uncommon but can occur. We may see a person who stood tall and strong at the funeral of a loved one, crying uncontrollably at the funeral of a distant relative. We may see someone unable to attend a memorial service because they claim it would be too difficult to face the widow. Grief can hit unexpectedly and seem all out of proportion to the situation. Displaced grief may need to be looked at carefully by friends and family in case professional help is required.

32

Listening to Our Hearts

Jane told us that a year after her husband died she began to feel as if she were losing her mind. She had been through so many experiences during the first year that at times it was overwhelming. For several days she kept having thoughts that plagued her about her sanity. It reached an almost unbearable fear around eight o'clock one evening, just as the phone rang.

A church friend apologetically said, "Jane, this may sound funny to you, but as I was praying I kept getting the idea to call you and tell you that you are not going crazy." She explained that she had hesitated about it, but the message was loud and clear. She laughingly added, "I guess you could say that I'm just following orders. Is there anything I can do for you?"

Jane had sighed with relief. There was nothing more this friend could do for Jane. She had brought the ultimate comfort with her call and message.

We must respond to these small, strange feelings we get even when we do not understand them. It is better to take a chance on sounding a bit odd than to miss an opportunity of divine intervention.

God knows about our suffering and works in his mysterious ways to send us help. Harold Blake Walker confirms this in his book *To Conquer Loneliness.*

Not long ago I was visiting with a courageous woman whose husband had been ill for more than a year. I remarked that through it all she had been a "good soldier." "Oh," she answered, "God has been my strength." Then she went on to say: "God works in strange ways. There were times when I thought I could not go on. Then the telephone would ring and somebody on the other end of the line would give me a needed lift. Or, maybe the doorbell would ring, and there would be someone I did not expect to see . . ."

Curiously, I never had thought of the woman in question as particularly religious, but there she was telling me that God had had a hand in the telephone calls that came at precisely the right moment and the ringing of the doorbell . . . and that in the deepest possible sense her prayers had been answered.

How blind we often are! Time and again in my ministry I have had a curious feeling I ought to go see somebody. There seemed to be no good reason for going, but I have learned to listen to those hunches. When I have gone I have found the reason for going, illness or trouble of one sort or another. Call my hunches what you will, I am altogether sure God has a hand in them. I am sure He has a hand in your strange feelings you ought to go here or there to be helpful.

God is mindful of the tears that flow and in a hundred ways He comes to share the hurt. He comes through the ministry of others and He comes to the inner sanctuary. When He comes, we are not afraid.[12]

33

Long-Distance Help

When our grieving friends or relatives live a great distance from us and we can not reach out and hug them, what can we do? We can write letters and we can phone.

Phone calls often prove to be difficult. The grieving person will begin to cry, making conversation almost impossible. This problem can be solved by asking if it is okay to pray with the individual. A simple prayer, spoken from the heart, soothes an aching soul. The time of prayer also allows the bereaved person the freedom to continue crying but does not end the conversation.

Further conversation is not necessary. The phone call has served its purpose. It has let the person know we are thinking about them and that we care.

34

Self-Care

One very important way to be of assistance to someone who is grieving is to keep ourselves in tip-top shape. A person who is grieving is often difficult to get along with and can be very wearing on the nerves. They will play the same "tapes" repeatedly, seem to cry over nothing, and demand our time when we least wish to be disturbed. Therefore it is important to take the time for ourselves so that we can be physically, emotionally, and spiritually ready with the strength to overcome any obstacles that might otherwise stand in the way of our wholehearted caring.

It is not selfish to take the time to read a humorous book or soak in a hot bubble bath. These are necessities that will relax us and replenish our own natural reserves so that we can be ready to share our time, energy, and other resources whenever necessary. An empty pitcher does little to quench a person's thirst.

We must remember to eat properly, get enough sleep, and take the time to exercise both our bodies and minds. We must seek others whom we can talk with, pray with, and be nourished by, so that we are in the best possible shape to help others. It is much more difficult to listen patiently to a grieving friend when our own head is throbbing with a headache because we did not take the time to eat breakfast. It is also difficult to listen to depressing stories constantly. However if they are balanced with good cheer and strong friendships they will not be as likely to drag us down. Support groups for people in helping professions are popping up in most communities.

I am part of a three-person prayer group. We meet each Monday morning for an hour or two of prayer when we lift each other up and pray over all aspects of each other's lives. Each week I walk away from these sessions filled with strength and confidence to face whatever the rest of the week might bring. "Where two or three gather together because they are mine, I will be right there among them." (Matt. 18:20) There is a special power in groups. Bereavement-support groups are recommended for the grieving but the helpers also need group contact to give them extra sustenance for their job as helper of the griever.

When a situation seems to be getting too heavy, a short respite can give renewed strength. Writer Arthur Gordon once said that salt water could cure anything, be it in the form of sweat, tears, or the ocean. I have thought about that solution and used it often. A good workout, a walk along the beach, or a good old-fashioned cry can send us back as better helpers.

I also treat myself to a long, leisurely bubble bath each night. I fill my oversized bathtub with fragrant bubbles and I soak until my skin gets wrinkly. I look forward to those quiet times that relax and refresh me. Another of my secrets is that I refuse to watch any television or movies that contain violence or depressing themes. I seek out light-hearted comedies, the sillier the better. Fortunately, I have been blessed with a family that has a great sense of humor. My husband and children fill our home with laughter over ridiculous antics. The fun we all have together restores us so that we are better able to face the rest of the outside world. We must never get so involved in helping others that we neglect our own good mental health, or eventually we will be unable to carry on in the helping capacity.

35

Providing Respect

Death brings about a feeling of low self-esteem, destroys self-confidence, and depletes energy. We can stand on the sidelines allowing grieving persons to draw on our self-esteem, confidence, and energy as they replenish their own supply. Ecclesiastes 4:9–12, reminds us:

> Two can accomplish more than twice as much as one, for the results can be much better. If one falls, the other pulls him up; but if a man falls when he is alone, he's in trouble. Also on a cold night two under the same blanket gain warmth from each other, but how can one be warm alone? And one standing alone can be attacked and defeated, but two can stand back-to-back and conquer; three is even better, for a triple braided cord is not easily broken.

The rewards of watching the growth and progress of someone who is grieving are infinite. To see a person in the lowest ebb of life who goes through a convalescent period to eventually reach full recovery is a miracle. The human spirit is too intricate to try to even understand. By being a caring presence we can assist with this recovery. We can be the one who helps them accomplish the tasks that need to be done, we can provide warmth, courage and help to fight off defeat. We can nurture the grieving person much as a gardener tends precious plants.

Margaret Jean Jones compares the human spirit to a shrub in her book *The World in My Mirror:* "A shrub that has been transplanted from the fertile soil of a nursery to a location with sandy soil suffers a great shock to its root system." The very roots of a grieving person are torn and exposed.

We can serve as the gardener who determines whether the plant lives and thrives or dies. If the plant is left unattended, it will become stunted and unattractive, unfruitful, and robbed of its potential—just like a grieving person left without support will react. However, with fertilizing, mulching, pruning, and watering, it can enrich its surroundings with its beauty and fruitfulness.

We will similarly be rewarded by the fruits that will be brought forth from a grieving person whom we have helped. If we are not a caring gardener, we take the chance of the person being plunged into the arid soil of tribulation. Choked by the weeds of self-pity and infested with depression, the human spirit soon becomes blighted and robbed of its potential. However, tended by a gardener and rooted in faith, nourished by the promises of Christ, and cultivated with trust, both the shrub or the griever can take hold and send out pruned branches stretching forth in new and better directions.

None of this happens overnight—with plants *or* people. Producing fruitfulness takes love, labor, care, and time. To be successful in our tending of grieving people, we must respect their individual rights. As a result of our care, we will see the growth and the beautiful blossoms.

Epilogue

Before working with grieving persons, I assumed that a year after the death the grief work was complete. Now I realize this is not possible. Grief will continue forever. There may be long periods of time in between the sadness, but then an unexpected wave will wash over us from time to time for the rest of our lives. *This is the price we pay for having loved someone. To never experience grief, we would have to never experience love.*

If we wish to help someone who is grieving, we must remember that grief goes on even after the first year. We can continue to mention the deceased person fondly, acknowledging the loss in our own life. We can continue to remember those special dates and holidays.

The second Christmas after the death is often worse than the first one. Family and friends that offered support the first year do not realize it is necessary the second year too. Plans that were carefully made the first year seem unnecessary, so the second Christmas creeps up without an armor of protection to cushion the impact. A caring friend can serve as that armor of protection by helping the grieving person plan ahead.

Often by the second year widows and widowers are dating. They are usually embarrassed to talk about their new social life. We should encourage them by letting them know we accept their new lifestyle. They should be made to feel comfortable with their choice and know we will continue to be their friend. Reaching out is a good sign. We need to let the bereaved know we realize that the lost loved one is not forgotten; instead it means that the bereaved person is adjusting successfully to their loss. Our reward is to watch grieving persons adjust and accept their altered life.

I recently received an invitation in an unfamiliar handwriting. With a puzzled look on my face, I opened it as I walked back to the house from the mailbox. It was from a widow who had been in one of our bereavement-support groups two years before. Apparently the group still continued to meet socially, and the members wanted me to join them for their two-year reunion dinner. I was delighted.

That evening I walked into a room of strangers. These could not possibly be the same people I had met two years ago. Those people had faced me with tears in their eyes, not smiles on their faces. This group was meticulously groomed, relaxed, and friendly. I remembered the tenseness I had felt as I walked into the room at our meetings, and the way the people would sit stiffly in their chairs with folded arms or clenched hands.

After exchanging hugs I sat down to join this group. What a wonderful time I had that night! Humorous stories were shared, local news topics were discussed, and occasionally someone would mention their lost loved one—not with sadness but with acceptance. We laughed together about one woman having to climb up on her roof to nail down shingles after a bad wind storm, and about our eighty-six-year-old gentleman's falling off a stepladder when he tried to change a light bulb. Amazingly he was completely unharmed from the fall. Practical tasks were no longer a problem. These people were functioning successfully in all areas.

I drove home from the dinner party with a light heart. I had received the best possible gift. I had been able to see an entire group of people who had come full circle in their grief work. It encouraged me to continue with my work and to write this book.

Appendix
Bill of Rights for the Bereaved

1. Do not make me do anything I do not wish to do.
2. Let me cry.
3. Allow me to talk about the deceased.
4. Do not force me to make quick decisions.
5. Let me act strange sometimes.
6. Let me see that you are grieving too.
7. When I am angry, do not discount it.
8. Do not speak to me in platitudes.
9. Listen to me, please!
10. Forgive me my trespasses, my rudeness, and my thoughtlessness.

Source Notes

Chapter 1 Responding to the News
1. Robert L. Veninga, *A Gift of Hope* (New York: Ballantine Books, 1985), p. 59.
2. Louise Carroll, "Be a Comfort," *LIVE*, September 27, 1987, p. 3.

Chapter 2 Offering Condolences
3. Donald P. McNeil, Douglas A. Morrison, and Henri J. M. Nouwen, *Compassion* (New York: Doubleday [Image Books], 1983), p. 13.
4. Ibid.

Chapter 3 Clichés
5. Adapted from Erin Linn, *I Know Just How You Feel . . . Avoiding the Clichés of Grief* (Barrington, Ill.: The Publisher's Mark, 1986), pp. 27, 43, 73, 85, 97, 100.

Chapter 8 The Forgotten Griever
6. Larry Richards and Paul Johnson, M.D., *Death and the Caring Community* (Portland, Ore.: Multnomah Press, 1980), p. 26.

Chapter 12 Sharing Memories

7. Barbara Bartocci, "Golden Scrapbooks of the Mind," *Reader's Digest,* December 1987, p. 87.

Chapter 15 The Symptoms of Grief

8. Alan D. Wolfelt, Ph.D., and Susan J. Wolfelt, M.D. "Medication and the Mourner: Understanding a Complex Issue," *Thanatos,* Fall 1987, p. 18.

Chapter 19 Listening Skills

9. Richards and Johnson, *Death and the Caring Community,* p. 125.

Chapter 27 A New Lifestyle

10. Verna Diggs, "Reflecting on Widowhood," *Upreach,* October 1987, p. 9.

Chapter 30 Reaching Out

11. J. Grant Swank, Jr., "The Bright Side of Pain," *Psychology for Living,* February 1986, p. 21.

Chapter 32 Listening to Our Hearts

12. Harold Blake Walker, *To Conquer Loneliness* (New York: Harper & Row, 1966), p. 141.

Suggested Reading List

The Courage to Grieve by Judy Tattlebaum, Harper & Row, 1980
A clearly written book on all aspects of grief and the resolution of it. Many self-help ideas.

Death, the Final Stage of Growth by E. Kubler-Ross, Prentice Hall, 1975
Discusses life and death. Theme is accepting our own death and that of others.

A Gift of Hope by Robert L. Veninga, Ballantine Books, 1985
Tells all about hope and what it means to an individual.

Good Grief by Granger Westburg, Fortress Press, 1962
Short, easy-to-understand book on the stages of grief.

A Grief Observed by C. S. Lewis, Bantam Books, 1973
Especially good for widowers. The journal of a famous author as he deals with the death of his wife.

How Do We Tell the Children? by Dan Schefer and Christine Lyons, Newmarket Press, 1986
Everything a person needs to know about dealing with death and children. Special crisis section for quick reference.

To Conquer Loneliness by Harold Blake Walker, Harper & Row, 1966
All about emotions, feelings, and life's stages.

Suggested Reading List

When Bad Things Happen to Good People by Harold S. Kushner, Avon, 1981
> A rabbi wrestles with the problems of human suffering. Some ideas are excellent; others are controversial.

When Will I Stop Hurting? by June Cerza Kolf, Baker, 1987
> Defines the stages of grief with reassurances of hope for the future.